Molokini

MOLOKINI

Hawai'i's Island Marine Sanctuary

By **MIKE SEVERNS**

and **PAULINE FIENE**

Photographed by **MIKE SEVERNS**

 ISLAND HERITAGE

Photo editing: David Pickell
Cover design: Danvers Fletcher
Book design and layout: David Pickell

Produced, published, and distributed by:

ISLAND HERITAGE
P U B L I S H I N G

94-411 Kōʻaki Street, Waipahu, Hawaiʻi 96797
Orders: (800) 468-2800 Information: (808) 564-8800
Fax: (808) 564 -8877
Website: **www.islandheritage.com**

First photo spread
A tiny wire coral goby (*Bryaninops yongei*) and a rare Lahaina ovulid (*Phenacovolva lahainaensis*) share a specialized habitat on a common wire coral (*Cirrhipathes anguina*). While the goby uses the coral as its home and a place to lay its eggs, the ovulid is a parasite, eating the coral tissue.

Second photo spread
A group of pyramid butterflyfish (*Hemitaurichthys polylepis*) have gathered on the reef to be cleaned by two Hawaiian cleaner wrasses (*Labroides phthirophagus*). The butterflyfish have raised their dorsal fins and spread their pectoral fins to make it easier for the wrasses to remove parasites.

Frontispiece
The wicked looking teeth and constantly open jaws of the colorful dragon moray (*Enchelycore pardalis*) make it appear menacing, but it is no more so than most other morays. The jaws cannot close because of their curve.

Contents

The habitat of the spectacular yellow anthias falls outside recreational diving depths. Before this photograph was taken in 1989, they had only been seen from submersibles, and were thought to live beyond the range of scuba divers. Yellow anthias live along the deep outer rim hovering close to the undersides of ledges and feeding on plankton.

HOLANTHIAS FUSCIPINNIS

Acknowledgments

Diving at Molokini and becoming acquainted with its myriad inhabitants over the last twenty years has been rewarding beyond imagination. The tutoring and assistance we've received from those who love the ocean and who specialize in this unique realm has added so much along the way.

John E. Randall, Senior Ichthyologist Emeritus at Bishop Museum on Oʻahu, opened a door for us to many scientific discoveries years ago, and generously continues to share his wealth of knowledge of fishes. David Sherrod, Geologist, USGS, Hawaiian Volcano Observatory; John Sinton, University of Hawaiʻi at Mānoa; and Chip Fletcher, University of Hawaiʻi at Mānoa, guided us as we pieced together the geological evidence to form a solid picture of Molokini's formation and geologic history. E. Alison Kay, University of Hawaiʻi at Mānoa, was an inspiration who taught a most valuable lesson: look for unusual habitats if you want to find unusual animals. James Maragos, Coral Reef Biologist, National Marine Fisheries Service on Oʻahu, surveyed and guided us in understanding the complicated coral reefs living at Molokini. Terrence Gosliner, California Academy of Sciences, shared his enthusiasm and knowledge of nudibranchs, joining us on dives at Molokini. Richard Pyle of Oʻahu taught us the basics of mixed gas diving and shepherded us on our first dives to the very base of Molokini—a high point in our years of diving there. Karin Meier of Oʻahu was an early supporter, locating reference material that was hard to find and cheering us on. Janie Culp of Oʻahu offered her expertise as a diver and researcher. In recent years Jennifer Anderson-Cymbaluk, Bo Lusher, Andy Schwanke, Dave Tanis, and Vici Tate of Maui have helped nail down coral spawning dates and have contributed their observations of marine life from thousands of hours underwater. Jennifer's discovery of *Octopus cyanea* nesting behavior in Hawaiʻi allowed us to learn of their reproductive pattern and to photograph their eggs.

Kealiʻi Reichel and Keliʻi Tauʻa, both Hawaiian scholars and chanters on Maui, interpreted the legends relating to Molokini and added depth to the words that have been written about the island. We are grateful to Keliʻi Tauʻa for translating and interpreting Molokini's legends in the essay presented here.

Camera maintenance and film processing also required special talents. Larry Orsendorf at Ikelite unwaveringly supported our lighting efforts to the tune of over fifty damaged pieces of equipment including strobes, strobe cords, strobe arms and electrical fittings for housings. Larry is best remembered for his, "You had it how deep?" when we were helping test a new strobe design. Randy Miller, Maui's camera repair guru, did whatever it took to get us back in the water. He cheerfully ad libbed when faced with equipment that had been taken deeper than designed or tested for, or pounded home in heavy seas on the deck of a boat. Rob Larsen supported us with professional services in developing and film, which may have often exceeded his authority.

Editing the entire manuscript was taken on by two very special people. John Hoover, librarian at the Hawaiʻi Medical Library on Oʻahu, took this job seriously and improved our work considerably. His enthusiastic correspondence concerning anything marine-related, and more significantly, concerning the subject of this book, brightened many of our days at the computer. He (and his books) have been invaluable resources.

Cory Pittman, a living legend among marine scientists who know him, also applied his editing expertise. His comments improved the text on many levels. He has been generous with his time and knowledge over many years, and has enhanced our marine experiences beyond measure.

The support of friends and family in a project like this was indispensable and fun. Rod and Ruth Dyerly cheered us on with wisdom and good humor from the beginning, often planning their dive vacations around our shooting needs. Martha and Morgan Hunter added incredible support, and were among our biggest fans. Jim and Roberta Fiene were usually the first to hear of any exciting discoveries and also reviewed the manuscript making valuable suggestions and corrections. Ruby and Robert L. Severns contributed whole-heartedly, offering both financial support (at one point in the form of a railway car which we sold to buy underwater photography equipment) and moral support for the difficult career we were heading toward.

We have been lucky to share dives at Molokini with thousands of divers and to have seen their delight and appreciation for Molokini's uniqueness. That sharing is perhaps the most satisfying of all.

Crown-of-thorns sea stars have unusual sharp venomous spines covering their back. Few predators can get past these spines and the sea star is therefore the perfect host for tiny sister shrimp, which may be yellow or maroon. The shrimp live on the sea star, feeding, mating, and carrying eggs until they hatch.
PERICLIMENES SOROR ON ACANTHASTER PLANCI

Introducing Molokini

From a distance, Molokini, the little wisp of an island off Maui's southwest shore, appears delicate and temporary; as if one big wave might submerge it forever. Half of the crater appears to be missing already, and it peaks only 160 feet above the surface of the sea. But this tiny islet is a giant in terms of the wildlife that it harbors. Rare plants cling to its crumbling slopes, seabirds roost and nest on its rocky cliffs, and a rapturous coral garden flourishes inside the crater. Leviathans, such as whales and whale sharks, occasionally pass by for cleaning or just out of curiosity. Thousands of reef fishes share the myriad habitats that are within and just outside the crater's protective arms.

The islet is one of Maui's more recent volcanic features. Formed 148,000 years ago, it is young compared to massive Haleakalā, which rose up 2 million years ago, but old relative to south Maui's most recent eruption about 500 years ago. Its location is fortunate. Positioned two and a half miles offshore in the ʻAlalākeiki Channel separating Maui and Kahoʻolawe, its reefs are relatively unaffected by runoff. Visibility in surrounding waters is consistently excellent—often over 160 feet.

Molokini has long been recognized as special. In the early 1900s, a visitor from Oahu raved about the coral garden he had seen in the crater. Thousands of visitors later, in 1977, the State of Hawaiʻi declared

The wave bench on the backside of Molokini is exposed to strong surge and wind erosion.

Molokini a Marine Life Conservation District, protecting it from most fishing and harvesting pressures. Recently, greater limits were placed on fishing. Now there is almost complete protection out to 100 yards from the island (trolling is still allowed within this buffer). These limits were imposed in recognition of the diverse marine life and Molokini's unique situation as Hawaiʻi's only island marine sanctuary.

From the surface, few would imagine how spectacular and diverse the marine life is below them. Living on the crater floor and along the rocky slopes of this little volcano are more than 260 species of reef fishes, 100 species of algae, and 38 species of hard corals. These are very impressive numbers given Molokini's size, just two-fifths of a mile from tip to tip. The cone rises from a 310-foot bottom, and its underwater habitats include sheer cliffs, rubbly slopes, shallow coral reefs, and sand channels. Many niches are available, and a great diversity of species occupies them. In addition, some animals are accustomed to divers and snorkelers as beings that will not harm them, so they are more easily approached and observed in feeding, courtship, and territorial displays.

Most residents and tour operators recognize that Molokini is unique and are in partnership to protect it. Boaters tie up to moorings, fish are not given handouts, divers and snorkelers are reminded to avoid contact with the reef, and the State of Hawaiʻi has begun monitoring coral coverage inside the crater. When combined with the excellent water quality and lack of sedimentation, Molokini's reefs and marine life should thrive for many years to come.

How Molokini Formed

A visit to the main Hawaiian Islands is full of views of massive mountain peaks, deep green valleys, and expansive black lava flows. How different then is the little tan islet of Molokini? Although other crescent-shaped islands exist in the Hawaiian chain, Lehua and Ka'ula in the rough waters near Ni'ihau to the west of Kaua'i, they are a long boat ride away and infrequently visited. Only Molokini is easily accessible to divers and snorkelers.

Molokini, Lehua, and Ka'ula are all tuff cones with only part of their broad crater rims visible above water. They owe their shape to the fact that water played a part in their formation, unlike the more familiar cinder cones that form on land. Cinder cones are visible from almost anywhere while driving around the islands. They typically result when lava from a deep subterranean conduit is ejected high into the air, as if shot from a gun. It falls back down closely around the vent as cinder, resulting in a rounded cone with a shallow bowl-shaped crater. Both tuff and cinder cones may form along cracks in a mountain. In the Hawaiian Islands they commonly occur in rough lines, like stepping stones leading down the mountain side and sometimes out to sea.

When a vent opens right along the coastline or just offshore, water influences the eruption. One of these was the scenario when Molokini formed. Similar eruptions in other parts of the world have shown us what it must have been like.

As red hot lava neared the opening of the conduit, it contacted cool ocean water that had either permeated the surrounding rock or flowed in when the vent opened. This created violent steam explosions that blasted the lava into particles of wet ash and ejected them in all directions at a relatively low trajectory. This formed Molokini's comparatively wide crater, two-fifths of a mile in diameter. At the same time, ash-laden steam shot hundreds of feet into the air to form a thick billowing column. Ash showered down, depositing a thin but distinct layer with each new explosion. Many thousands of these layers eventually created a cone roughly 500 feet in height from its base on the ocean floor to its summit above the waves. When viewed closely, the layers are easily visible both above and below water.

These ash layers raise the question of where sea level stood at the time of Molokini's formation. Layered deposits can form under a variety of conditions, both as lava flows underwater and as ash deposits in air. Because Molokini's layers are thinly-bedded—as ash layers would be—all the way to the base of the cone 310 feet underwater, without the slightest change in appearance, we suspect that they all formed as wet ash landing upon the previous deposit above water. This hypothesis means that sea level would have had to have been roughly 310 feet lower during formation than at present. This fits well with the recent potassium-argon dating of Molokini, which put its age at 148,000 years old, plus or minus 17,000 years. During that period, sea level was sufficiently low to accommodate this theory. Maui's coastline would have extended much farther out to sea, putting Molokini along the coastline or within one mile of shore when it erupted.

While Molokini was forming, it is clear that the wind was blowing from the north-northwest and the greatest amount of ash landed along the southern rim. This built a lopsided cone, higher on the downwind side where the majority of airborne ash was deposited. Today it might appear that half of

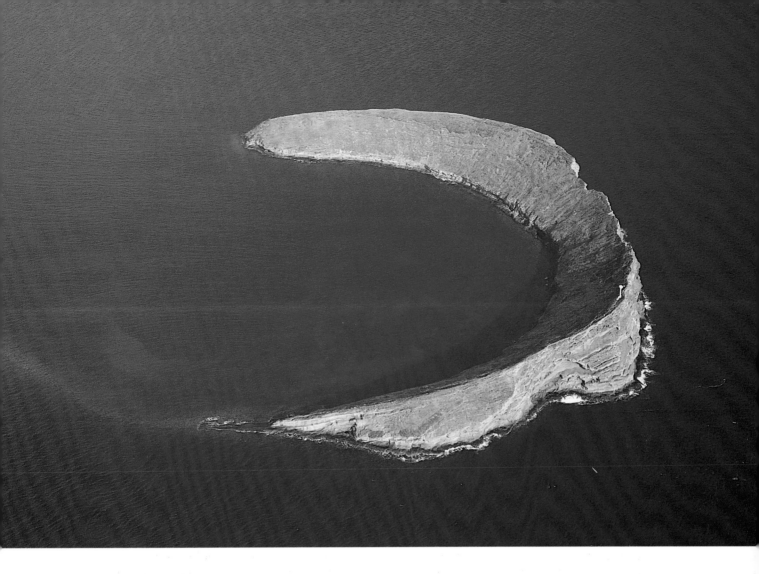

Molokini's rim has fallen away, but since no talus, landslide blocks, or lava flows exist at the base of the north flank, it appears that the rim never formed a complete circle.

An aerial view of the island, however, reveals that there is more to the crater rim than the half-circle visible above the ocean's surface. The western tip of the crescent continues underwater, extending the rim to three-quarters of a circle in total. This part of the rim is only about three feet deep at its shallowest point, and was submerged when the sea rose to cover it, roughly 6,000 years ago. Today this submerged part of the rim has been populated by thousands of coral colonies, which thrive in the sunlight and constantly moving water just a few feet below the surface.

After formation, Molokini may have stood more than 500 feet high from its base to its summit, a wind-shaped cone composed of many layers of soft ash. As rainwater percolated down through the ash, chemical reactions occurred, mobilizing and regrouping

Although at first glance it appears that Molokini Island has lost part of its crater rim due to erosion, geologists believe the little cinder cone was lopsided from the beginning. They argue that incessant blowing of the trades carried the ash to the south and southwest. The crater, formed from layers of compacted and cemented ash, seems to have arisen about 148,000 years ago.

various compounds. This cemented the ash into a harder substance called tuff. Some of the layers contained finer-grained ash than others, and a harder tuff was achieved due to the greater surface area available for the chemical reactions. These harder layers may be seen as small steps on the inner slope of the island and as prominent strata underwater.

The sea level has risen and fallen many times during the still-ongoing transformation from an ash cone into a harder tuff cone. Sometimes the rate of rise and fall has

For several thousand years, waves have cut into the south side of Molokini (above) carving a large notch or wave-cut bench. At 240 feet underwater (below) lies a similar notch, which was cut by waves when the sea level was that much lower. A large black coral tree grows in the dark space of the old wave bench.

been quick and sometimes it has been slower, on several occasions pausing long enough for wave action to carve well-defined notches into the cone at various depths. The deepest and most striking of these is a notch 250 feet underwater. However, because of the possible subsidence of Molokini, there is no way to know what sea stand might have carved the notch and when. Other less-defined ledges were carved at 130 feet and at 60 feet around the outside of the cone as the sea level briefly stabilized. The large, beautiful notch carved by recent levels of the sea can be viewed all around the crater rim, although it is more pronounced along the outer rim where wave action is greater.

Wave action, rain, and wind are all at work on Molokini, eroding it away before our eyes. Because of its location in the middle of the ʻAlalākeiki Channel, it has no true leeward side. Tradewinds funneling through the valley between Haleakalā and west Maui hit it from the north, out of Māʻalaea; easterly winds, wrapping around the southern coast of Maui, come at it from the south. The north side (the inner crescent) is the better preserved because large ocean swells from the north are blocked by the island of Maui. The south side (the outer rim) is the more severely eroded due to large storm waves rolling in from the open ocean. Cutting deeply into the island, the waves undermine the rock above, which falls away leaving sheer cliffs along the back side of the island. Wind and rain remove any softer material, giving the cliffs their moth-eaten appearance.

The rocks, boulders, and flakes that continue to slip from the cliffs and ledges tumble into the ocean creating new habitat for small marine creatures. As rain and wind eat away at the tuff, birds are increasingly able to burrow into the crumbling rock. Eventually, however, Molokini will play herself out and erode to meet the sea. The sheer weight of the Maui/Kahoʻolawe/Lanaʻi complex will cause further subsidence as it carries Molokini down with it. For a time, a small coral-covered bank may exist but exposure during future ice ages will probably erode it completely away. Until that distant time, however, Molokini will continue to be a scenic wonder, both above and below the sea.

Molokini Islet 1:3,500

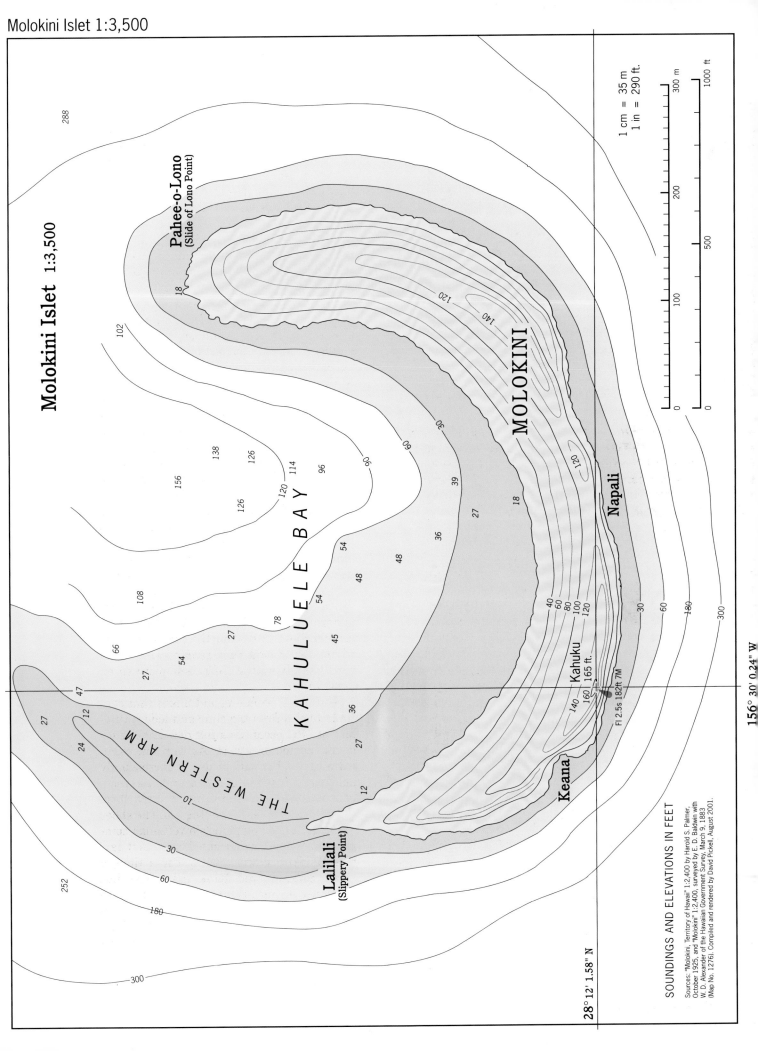

Molokini Islet 1:3,500

Pahee-o-Lono
(Slide of Lono Point)

288

102

138
156
126
114
126
120
96
108
66
78
27
54
252
27
47
12
24
27
10
30
60
180
300

KAHULUELE BAY

THE WESTERN ARM

Lalilali
(Slippery Point)

Keana

Kahuku
165 ft.
140
160
182ft 7M
Fl 2.5s

Napali

MOLOKINI

120
140
120
120
30
60
30
60
180
300
40
60
80
100
120

18
27
36
39
30
60
90
45
54
48
54
54
12
27
36
18

28° 12' 1.58" N

156° 30' 0.24" W

SOUNDINGS AND ELEVATIONS IN FEET

1 cm = 35 m
1 in = 290 ft.

300 m
1000 ft

Sources: "Molokini, Territory of Hawaii" 1:2,400 by Harold S. Palmer,
October 1925, and "Molokini" 1:2,400, surveyed by E. D. Baldwin with
W. D. Alexander of the Hawaiian Government Survey, March 9, 1883
(Map No. 1276). Compiled and rendered by David Pickell, August 2001.

Molokini in Legend

By Keli'i Tau'ā

Molokini, a needle between the sacred island of Kaho'olawe and magical Maui, today serves as a beacon for all who pass by. Snorkelers, divers, canoe paddlers, and others who decide to stop, get an opportunity to feel the aura surrounding the island, perhaps even receiving a little jolt from the *mana* (spiritual power) that exists there.

Few miniature islands in the Hawaiian archipelago inspired *kūpuna* (elders) of the past to bestow as many place names. However, this infant island not only presents a handful of place names, but also provides stories that connect the places with the four major Hawaiian gods, Lono, Kū, Kanaloa, and Kāne.

Pahe'e o Lono is located on the east point of the crescent, Kahu Kū sits in the middle, and Kāne and Kanaloa, according to the chant *Mele a Pāku'i*, contributed indirectly to the island's mythical creation. Excerpts from the chant, *'O Wākea Kahiko Luamea* (opposite page), suggest that earth mother Papa first gave birth to the island Hawai'i, then crossed the rough channel of 'Alenuihāhā with morning sickness to create Maui. Continuing, with help from the gods Kāne and Kanaloa, Papa delivered Mololani (Molokini) in the 'Alalākeiki (wailing child) Channel, and finally created the sacred island of Kaho'olawe.

In another *oli* (chant), the storyteller connects the birth of Molokini to the birth of nearby Kaho'olawe. In this story, after Kaho'olawe was born, its *'iewe* (placenta) was cut by Uluhina, who tossed it into the sea where it became the islet of Molokini.

> Ki'ina aku Uluhina,
> Moku ka piko o ke kamaiki,
> Ka'iēwe o ke keiki i lele
> I komo i loko o ka 'ape nalu;
> Ka'ape'ape kai 'ale'ale,
> Loa'a ka malo o ke kama
> O Molokini ka moku

He 'iēwe ia —a—,
He 'iēwe ka moku...

Uluhina then was called upon,
The navel of the little one was cut
The afterbirth of the child that was
> *thrown*
Into the folds of the rolling surf;
The froth of the heaving sea,
Then was found the loin cloth for the
> *child*
Molokini the island
is the navel string,
The island is the navel string...

In ancient times, the placenta of a newborn was carefully washed, then buried to prevent evil-doers from molesting it. However, if the parents wanted a newborn son to be a seafarer, the cord was taken out and dropped into the ocean. Such could have been the desire of Uluhina. Alongside Kaho'olawe and Molokini is the Kealai-Kahiki Channel, whose name means "the path to Kahiki (Tahiti)." Thus, those who were born to be seafarers and had their *'iewe* tossed into the KealaiKahiki Channel were blessed with an ocean path back to Kahiki.

Stories of *kupua* (demigods) that roamed the land and sea abound in Hawai'i. In the next *mo'olelo* (legend) of Molokini, several *kupua* (demigods) are involved in a love triangle, but let me start by describing the central character of this story, the *mo'o* (lizard).

The word *mo'o* shows up in some very important Hawaiian words, such as *mo'okū'auhau* (genealogical pedigree), *mo'olau* (many lizard gods or having many descendants), *mo'olelo* (story, tale, myth, history, tradition), and *mo'opuna* (grandchild). *Mo'o* itself means lizard, reptile of any kind, dragon, serpent and/or water spirit. Now let us return to the love story.

Pu'u o kali (lizard mother) and Pu'u hele (lizard father) were *kupua* that took the

ʻO Wākea Kahiko Luamea

ʻO Papa, ʻo Papahānaumoku ka wahine	*Papa who gave birth to islands the wife*
Hānau Tahiti kū, Tahiti moe	*Tahiti-east, Tahiti-west*
Hānau Kaʻāpapanuʻu	*Born the highest level*
Hānau Keʻāpapalani	*Born the sky level*
Hānau Hawaiʻi	*Born Hawaiʻi*
Ka moku makahiapo	*The firstborn island*
Ka makahiapo a lāua	*The firstborn child of them*
ʻO Wākea lāua ʻo Kāne	*Of Wākea and Kāne*
ʻO Papa ʻo Walinuʻu ka wahine	*Papa and Walinuʻu the wife*
Hoʻokauhua Papa i ka moku	*Papa conceived the island*
Hoʻīloli iā Maui	*Was morning-sick with Maui*
Hānau Mauiloa he moku	*Born Mauiloa an island*
I hānau iā he alo lani	*Was born with chiefly countenance*
He uʻilani-uʻilani	*A handsome high chief*
Hei kapa lau māewa	*Treated with sacred respect*
He nui Mololani no Kū, no Lono	*Mololani (Molokini) was great for Kū, for Lono*
No Kāne mā lāua ʻo Kanaloa	*For Kāne and Kanaloa*
Hānau kapu ke kuakoko	*Born during sacred pains*
Kaʻahea Papa iā Kanaloa he moku	*Papa was prostrate with Kanaloa, an island*

shape of *puʻu* (hills) at Māʻalaea on the island of Maui. Their *kahiapo* (firstborn) was a lizard girl named Puʻu o inaina. The parents recognized that she was a special girl so they placed her on the sacred island of Kahoʻolawe. She became the wife of two brothers, Kaʻakakai (the older) and Kaʻanahua (the younger). Food and water were scarce on the island so the two brothers relocated to the Kahalawai Mountains at Hanaʻula on Maui, leaving the young girl by herself.

The brothers became *kanaka mahiʻai* (farmers) so as to furnish their wife with food. They planted and harvested their crops and cooked the food before delivering it to their wife, Puʻu o inaina, and to their parents-in-law. In their demigod bird form, the two flew to the different locations to deliver their food.

During the moments of separation, Kaʻakakai and Kaʻanahua longed for their beautiful wife, but their commitment to supply the family with food and water kept them apart from her. Meanwhile the loneliness of Kahoʻolawe got to Puʻu o inaina and

she ventured off to Māʻalaea to meet with the handsome Lohiʻau, chief of Kauaʻi and husband of Pele.

Eventually, word of the heated love affair of Puʻu o inaina and Lohiʻau drifted up the slopes of Kanaio to Kahiki Nui where Pele was temporarily residing. Upon hearing of the adultery of the two, Pele sent a powerful curse down the mountain to Kahoʻolawe where Puʻu o inaina resided. Upon receiving this high-powered imprecation, the lovely young woman was consumed by guilt. In an attempt to escape her remorse, she hurriedly departed from Kahoʻolawe by jumping into the sea of Kanaloa.

There were several possible reasons for her to have done this. The first was to cleanse herself in the ocean water as many Hawaiians do today. Secondly, since Pele represents fire, the ocean might have provided a protective shield. Thirdly, her supernatural power to change into a water spirit might have been a means of escaping the wrath of Pele.

Due to the adulterous event that occurred, Pele decided to go to meet her

From ʻUlupalakua on Maui you can see the cinder cone Puʻu olaʻi (the lizard's tail) in the foreground, Molokini (the lizard's head) in the channel, and the island of Kahoʻolawe in the distance.

lover Lohiʻau at Keālia, Kamāʻalaea. As she descended from Kahiki Nui, she was blocked by Puʻu hele, Puʻu o inaina's protective father. Pele survived the *moʻo* encounter and moved down to the ocean's edge. There she disguised herself before walking into the water. To her surprise she saw the adulterous Puʻu o inaina, her *moʻo* body stretched out from Kahoʻolawe to Maui. With all the strength and jealous hate in her, she cut Puʻu o inaina in two, leaving her head as the semicircular island of Molokini and her tail as Puʻu olaʻi at Mākena.

Today, supporting Puʻu olaʻi inshore are three surrounding ridges with *moʻo* names. They are Moʻoiki (short ridge); Moʻoloa (long ridge); and Moʻomoku (severed ridge). The ridges serve as protection from any inland assault of Puʻu olaʻi, and Kahoʻolawe shields Molokini from foreign aggression.

Another short story about the remote island originates from Haʻupu, a hill on Molokaʻi. There was a battle at the hill, led by a *kupua* named Kana. When Kana exerted force upon the enemy, the hill responded by growing upwards into the heavens. The hill and Kana continued to grow in size until Kana outgrew the hill, sending fear into his enemies. Kana then trod the hill, breaking it into small pieces. Some fragments of the hill flew over to the Koʻolau Mountains of Oʻahu. Other pieces fell close to Molokaʻi, and other pieces sailed to Maui to form Molokini.

Two of Molokini's place names passed down through *kupuna*, Lalilali and Keana, remain a mystery. The legend might still be sailing yonder as part of the pieces that broke from Haʻupu to form other *moʻo* islands in ʻAlalākeiki Channel. Let the wailing of the keiki, and the mana of the four major Hawaiian gods with the lei of Kanaloa, direct us to the hidden wonders of Molokini.

Hawaiian Uses of Molokini

In addition to Molokini's place in Hawaiian legend, it was also a great resource for fishing and probably even birding. Because Molokini is usually spared the northeasterly tradewinds until mid-day, it offers fairly reliable calm water in the morning. The predictability of the daily weather, the certainty of excellent fishing, and the seasonal availability of nesting seabirds made it an important resource for the villagers living along the nearby coast.

Offshore rocks and islets are favorite breeding and roosting areas for seabirds due to their lack of predators and proximity to the open ocean. Hawaiians are known to have harvested such areas. Although Molokini's steep slopes are difficult to negotiate, they would have allowed access to the island's large colony of wedge-tailed shearwaters during the March through August nesting season. Now that Molokini is a seabird sanctuary, the population has recovered and several thousand birds reside there.

Unlike the fully recovered seabird populations, we can only guess what the extent of Molokini's underwater resources was before modern fishing and trolling took their toll. Hawaiian fishermen probably had far less impact on its marine resources than modern fishermen, even though they fished a wide variety of marine life as evidenced by lost tackle. Stone sinkers of various types lost on the bottom offer clues to the creative strategies devised by early Hawaiians to exploit Molokini's varied marine habitats.

In protected water along the inner rim are found small carved stone sinkers shaped like bread loaves—a shape unique to the Hawaiian Islands. These were often attached to several types of nets constructed of *olonā* fiber from the bark of a native shrub. One particularly ingenious net, a shallow square dip net called *'upena uhu*, was used for catching large parrotfishes. The bread loaf sinkers were fitted to the ends of two crossed sticks which acted as spreaders for the net. The net was attached by the corners to the ends of two downward-arching crossed sticks. A cord was tied at the crossing and the net was dropped to the bottom. The net fisherman would catch a parrotfish, or *uhu*, using a baited hook. Then he would keep it alive as a decoy and lower it to the bottom over the net to attract other parrotfish. When a parrotfish approached the decoy, the fisherman, viewing from the surface, hauled the net up quickly. Fishermen knew that parrotfishes would always swim downward toward the safety of the reef when trying to escape. The combined effect of the fish swimming downward and the fisherman pulling the net up bent the slender sticks downward, drawing the corners of the net together and trapping the parrotfish.

Inside the crater, divers occasionally see other sinker stones, shaped like a coffee bean and about the size of one's palm. These were once part of octopus lures called *leho he'e* (see below). A fisherman would lash a carved bone barb to a wooden shank to create a hook. He then sandwiched the end of the shank between a cowrie shell (the lure) and the coffee bean-shaped stinker stone, often

OCTOPUS LURE
leho he'e or *ipo*

attaching strips of ti leaf behind the barb as a skirt. Before lowering the lure to the bottom, the fisherman in his canoe might spread oily bits of chewed *kukui* nut on the surface of the sea. This would make it glassy and enable him to see down to about 100 feet. Finding a likely area he lowered the lure to the bottom and pulled it along slowly, occasionally jerking it up and down to attract the attention of an octopus. Seeing the desirable cowrie, the octopus would move quickly across the bottom, enveloping the cowrie

Carved sinker stones such as this one laying on the bottom at Molokini give clues to the different fishing practices used here by early Hawaiians. This breadloaf-shaped sinker, unique to the Hawaiian islands, was used as a net sinker.

with its tentacles. The fisherman would then yank the line, hook the octopus, and bring it to the surface. So tight was the embrace of the octopus, and so oblivious was the animal to everything else, that the hook was often not even necessary. The tenacious embrace of the octopus did not go unnoticed by the Hawaiians who called this lure *ipo*, meaning "lover." As an example of the depth of Hawaiian knowledge, the cowrie shells were attached in a way that made them easy to change depending on the different periods of the day!

Smooth beachworn stones laying on the bottom off the outer rim are evidence of yet another fishing practice. Stones of this type do not occur naturally at Molokini. Hawaiians brought them for *palu* fishing, a method which took advantage of the some-times strong current running along the outer slopes. First, the fisherman would bait a hook and wrap it in a cloth-like sheath of coconut leaf containing *palu* (chum). The *palu was* made from strong-smelling fish parts ground up with oils, plant products, and octopus ink. He then tied a smooth beach stone to the package, using a few turns of line and a slip knot. Finally he lowered the package to the bottom, raised it

slightly, and yanked the cord. The stone dropped, the package opened, and the *palu* was carried down current, attracting fish to his baited hooks. This allowed fishermen to draw fish from a much larger area than would otherwise have been possible.

For fishing the deeper waters of the outer rim, fishermen used a large teardrop shaped sinker stone called *pōhākialoa*, or "long stone." The shape of this plummet sinker was peculiar to the Hawaiian Islands; swollen at the base, tapering to a neck, and ending in a very small knob around which line was tied. Up to 10 inches long and weighing as much as seven pounds, these sinkers could drop fishing lines in deep water far more quickly than smaller sinkers, especially if a current were running. Divers have seen them as deep as 180 feet on Molokini's outer slopes.

The old Hawaiians' intimate knowledge of marine habitats and their highly special-ized fishing techniques astound us, even today, and demonstrate their lineage as sea-faring people of unmatched skill. While Hawaiians no longer fish at Molokini, their presence will always be felt, as their lost sinker stones appear and disappear in the shifting sand.

Recent History of Molokini

Although Molokini was a part of the lives of Hawaiians, who lived nearby for over 1,500 years, it seems to have escaped the notice of English navigator Captain James Cook's crew as they skirted Kahoʻolawe after his death on the island of Hawaiʻi in 1775. Europeans learned of it a decade later when French explorer Jean-Françoise de Galoup, Compte de La Perouse, charted its location in 1786. In 1883, King David Kalakaua hired two American engineers, E.D. Baldwin and Arthur C. Alexander, to survey the island. Shortly thereafter Molokini was officially included in the charted Hawaiian Islands.

Since that time, Molokini has interested people for many different reasons. Plants have colonized the islet in spite of scanty soil, steep slopes, and daliy exposure to strong trade winds. At last count, 56 species grew here, 38 percent of them native to Hawaiʻi. These include a few rare plants believed to be extinct on the main islands due to introduced predators. Because these predators are absent on Molokini, a few native species have been able to survive. One, a succulent recognized as a new species by Robert Hobdy, was named for the island as *Portulaca molokiniensis*. It also survives on Kahoʻolawe and on one of its islets, Puʻu koaʻe.

Also taking advantage of Molokini's isolation, birds crowd its predator-free slopes (although grapsid crabs remain a possible predator of small hatchlings). In 1980, a Hawaiʻi Audubon Society survey reported two species of birds nesting on the island in impressive numbers, wedge-tailed shearwaters and Bulwer's petrels. An estimated 1,500 nesting pairs dig their burrows in the crumbling rock, the majority being shearwaters. In the evening, just after the sun has set, the birds return from a day of fishing at sea and, finding their burrows in the darkness, waddle in to feed the day's catch to their chicks.

More conspicuous are the occasional brown boobies and the seasonal gathering of great frigatebirds, both of which use the island to roost at night but do not nest here. The great frigatebird, which has a wingspan of seven feet, is called ʻiwa (thief) by Hawaiians. Its technique is to harass other fish-eating birds in flight, using its superior size and maneuverability, until the other bird drops or regurgitates its fish in terror. The frigatebird then swoops down and snatches the falling fish out of the air. These majestic birds never land at sea but return to roost on the inner slopes at night, and are still in place when the first charter boats arrive in the morning. Later in the day they may be seen soaring high above the crater. The distinct, white guano streaks that they produce are visible for months after the gathering leaves. Although people are forbidden from setting foot on the islet (Molokini has been a state-managed seabird sanctuary for 22 years), its varied bird life can be seen from a boat by careful watchers during morning and evening hours.

Other than birds and a skink, the only vertebrate animals known to have inhabited Molokini are rabbits. Introduced prior to 1915, possibly to breed and provide food for some Maui residents, they were still present in 1961 but died out shortly thereafter.

Molokini's position in the middle of a shipping lane, the ʻAlalākeiki Channel, called for a navigation light to be erected, and the first one was installed in 1911. During World War II it was extinguished for security reasons, and ultimately destroyed by bombardiers who used Molokini for target practice. When the war ended a wooden light tower was erected which lasted 42 years until a storm brought it down. A stainless steel tower was constructed afterward and is now serviced by helicopter by the U.S. Coast Guard.

As a practice target, Molokini did not sustain much damage, although it was certainly altered somewhat in appearance. Other small islets and offshore rocks were targeted during this time as well, and some of these were obliterated by explosives. At Molokini, bombing and strafing left impact craters

FREGATA MINOR

PORTULACA MOLOKINIENSIS

During the summer months, great frigatebirds (left) roost on the inner slopes of Molokini at night. A superior flying machine capable of outmaneuvering any other seabird in competition for fish, the frigate bird harasses other seabirds until they drop or regurgitate their food, which the frigate recovers from the air. Recently recognized as a new species, the Molokini Portulaca (below left) is known from only two other places—Kahoʻolawe and one of its offshore islets, Puʻu koaʻe. In these isolated pockets it has survived, while disappearing from the main islands long ago. Strips of sponge-covered metal (opposite) are all that is left of a bomb, a reminder of a time when Molokini was not treasured for its marine life. Fifty years ago, the island was used as a target for practicing Navy bombardiers.

and twisted metal on the inner slopes, and bullets embedded in the outer cliffs. Use of the island for target practice may explain why numbers of large seabirds were not recorded from Molokini until recently.

Bombs landed in the water as well. With increased recreational use of the island, the U.S. Navy became concerned about unexploded ordnance left from years of bombing. In 1975, the Navy detonated two large bombs inside the crater, pulverizing a large area of coral reef—damage still visible today. When plans for future detonations were announced in 1984, divers took the matter into their own hands and successfully dragged several bombs into deeper water. Later that year, the Navy proceeded with detonations in spite of local opposition. Four years later, after much public outcry, the Navy removed some of the remaining bombs by lifting them off the bottom and towing them into deeper water, beyond scuba diving limits. Others were left and a few can still be seen while diving at Molokini.

Black coral was harvested commercially from Molokini beginning in the late 1950s until 1977, when Molokini was made a Marine Life Conservation District. Deepwater divers reduced dense stands of black coral to stumps, which remain today to remind us of its former abundance. In the quarter century since harvesting stopped, small black coral trees have begun to recolonize the walls. One day they will again impress us with their size and numbers.

In light of heightened interest in the health of coral reefs in Hawaiʻi, Molokini's coral coverage is now being monitored by the State of Hawaiʻi Division of Aquatic Resources, the Hawaiʻi Institute of Marine Biology, and the University of Hawaiʻi Marine Options Program. Video is taken regularly along permanent transects within the crater and the percentage of coral cover in each area will eventually be able to be compared over many years.

Molokini deserves all the protection that can be given. Taking anything naturally occurring, whether living or dead, is prohibited within 100 yards of the island. Bottom fishing is also not allowed within 100 yards, but unfortunately trolling is still permitted within the preserve boundaries. Moorings have been installed within the crater so that boats need not anchor in fragile habitat. Once mooring installation is complete, all anchoring will be prohibited. Molokini has given great pleasure to many people, from the one-time visitor to those who make a living sharing its beauty with others. Any protective measures are well placed.

A male bullethead parrotfish or uhu *darts over the reef. Using only their pectoral fins, parrotfish in general are surprisingly fast swimmers, particularly during territorial disputes and courtship activities.*

CHLORURUS SORDIDUS

Center Reef

Protected from the surf by the curve of the crater rim, a stunning climax coral reef thrives inside the bay, interspersed with channels of pure white sand.

Eighty-four years ago the fledgling *Maui News* printed a note from the secretary of the Hawai'i Tuna Club, newly returned to O'ahu from a Maui fishing trip. In the submerged crater of Molokini, he reported, lies the "greatest coral garden anywhere in Hawai'i." Since his visit, the beauty of Molokini's reefs have impressed many divers and snorkelers. More important than its visual effect, however, is the habitat it creates for thousands of fishes and other marine creatures, providing both food and shelter. These extensive coral beds within the crescent owe their continuing health to Molokini's offshore location, its frequent currents, and to the protection offered by its rim.

Over two miles offshore, Molokini is far removed from the sediment that washes into the ocean from Maui. The island itself is a rock with no soil to speak of on its steeply sloping sides. These factors result in unusual water clarity which allows sunlight to penetrate easily, feeding the symbiotic algae that live within the corals' tis-

Holding one of its "large" claws in front of its head, this little bumblebee shrimp clings to the spines of a collector urchin, hāwa'e po'o hina. This species of shrimp has evolved to precisely match the coloration and pattern of the spines. It feeds on organic matter that catches on the urchin's spines and on the skin that covers the spines themselves.

sues. The offshore location also means that Molokini experiences stronger currents which bring food and sweep away any potential sediment.

Protected from surf on three sides by the rim of the crater and on the remaining side by the island of Maui, the coral reef in the center of the crater thrives. Along most Hawaiian coasts corals are subjected to periodic destruction by surf. This opens up new habitat in which ever-shifting combinations of coral species settle, compete, and grow. Because the reef in the center of the crater is seldom disturbed, the coral colonies already present have reached a balance and the percentages of different species remains roughly the same. Called a climax coral reef, this one is dominated by two species of corals: rice coral (*Montipora capitata*) and spreading coral (*Montipora patula*), a combination rarely seen in Hawai'i.

Rice coral releases its eggs and sperm annually on summer nights. Small bundles containing eggs and sperm are released by the coral and rise slowly to the surface. There they mix and unite, creating the next generation of coral. Because of the high concentration of rice coral inside Molokini, this spawning event is a phenomenal sight with many thousands of pink bundles the size of small bubbles rising like a beaded curtain.

Seen from above, the sea floor inside the crater appears to be in motion with alternating swirls of dark coral reef and wisps of

The colorful feeding and respiratory tentacles of this Christmas tree worm (left) seem to invite predators to take a bite, but at the slightest indication of a threat, they are yanked in. Then a calcareous trap door is slammed shut, leaving a sharp spine at the entrance to the worm hole to greet attackers. Tiny brushlike teeth allow the ornate butterflyfish or kīkākapu (below) to snip off the extended tentacles of coral polyps. After one bite, the surrounding polyps withdraw their tentacles, and the butterflyfish moves on. Only the tentacles are eaten, and they regenerate. During the day, yellowfin goatfish or weke ʻula (right) school in protective balls, but curiosity seems to have lured these three from the safety of the crowd.

WORM: SPIROBRANCHUS GIGANTEUS
CORAL: PORITES LOBATA

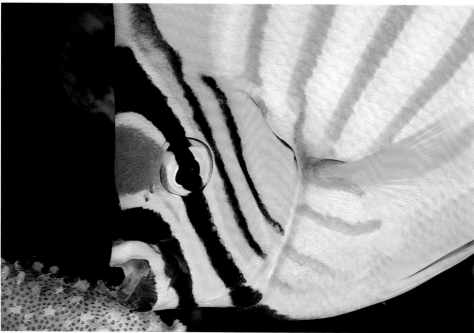

BUTTERFLYFISH: CHAETODON ORNATISSIMUS; CORAL: POCILLOPORA EYDOUXI

MULLOIDICHTHYS VANICOLENSIS

bright blue sand channels. Imperceptibly, it *is* in motion. As the corals are abraded by parrotfishes, bored into by sea snails and worms, and worn by the movement of waves, the coral skeletons are broken down into particles that sift through the reef and flow into the sand channels at the edges. The sand, ever so slowly, then flows down the slope and out the mouth of the crater.

Molokini's sand is noticeably whiter than Maui's coastal sand due to a much larger percentage of marine animal particles and fewer grains of volcanic origin. On a calm day the sand is easily visible from a boat above, and a snorkeler on the surface can discern many of the sand's inhabitants. Big black sea cucumbers, feeding in their laboriously slow ritual, are scattered across the bottom. Meandering tracks and furrows on the sand's surface betray various sea snails plowing through underneath. Ropy mounds indicate the presence of large sand-dwelling worms which ingest quantities of sand, filter out the nutrients, then eject it on the surface.

Divers have the opportunity for a closer view: a crab can be seen living a protected life inside the mouth of a sea cucumber; a

snail's furrow can be followed to its end and uncovered to reveal the snail in its shell; the ropy mound grows slowly as the worm ejects the processed sand. Divers can also search for camouflaged fishes such as flounders, which match their colors to the sand, and burrowing eels, which expose only their heads. Many octopuses, crabs, and shrimps live beneath the sand by day, emerging only at night. Goatfishes hunt some of these sand-dwellers by day, plying the sand with a pair of tentacles called barbels which detect chemicals given off by their prey. The spectacular flying gurnard disturbs the sand with its finger-like pelvic fins flushing out small fishes and crustaceans.

Acres of healthy coral reef, interrupted by winding sand channels, make the center of the crater a delight to explore. In the late morning or early afternoon, when the sun is high, the coral "dances" with the movement of light rays breaking through the surface of the ocean. Embraced by the arms of the crater rim, the coral gardens and sand channels offer a fascinating assemblage of habitats that would take many days to explore and many lifetimes to understand.

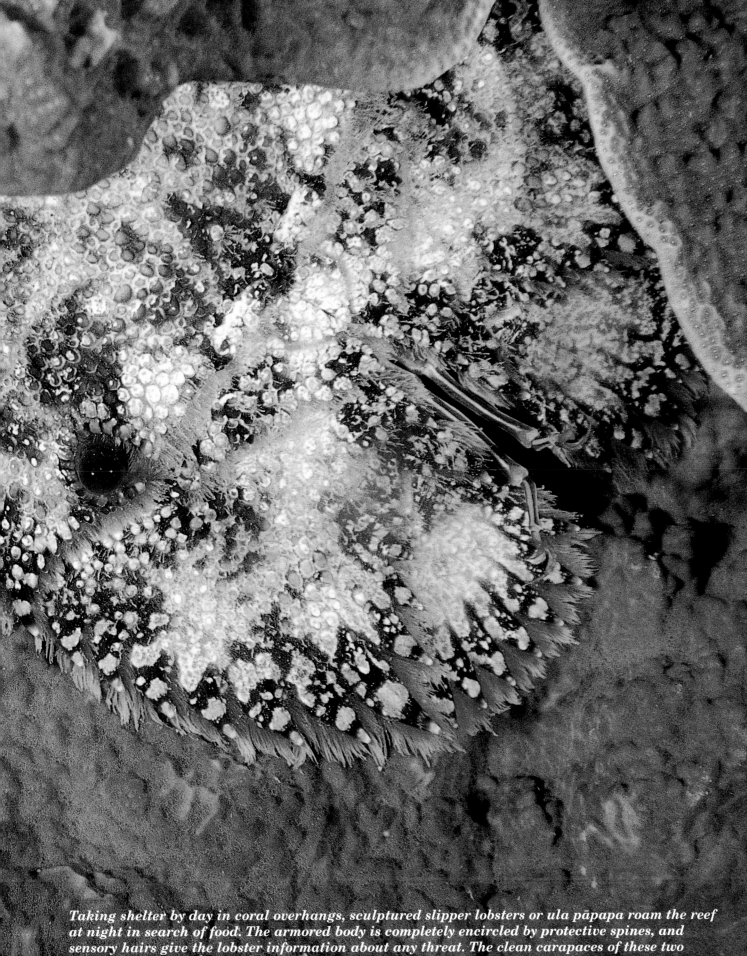

Taking shelter by day in coral overhangs, sculptured slipper lobsters or ula pāpapa roam the reef at night in search of food. The armored body is completely encircled by protective spines, and sensory hairs give the lobster information about any threat. The clean carapaces of these two suggest they have recently molted.

LOBSTERS: PARRIBACUS ANTARCTICUS; CORAL: PORITES RUS

CYPRAEA TALPA

TRIAENODON OBESUS

The shell of the mole cowrie (above) is kept glossy and free of colonizing organisms by the snail's mantle, which usually completely covers the shell. Contractions in the muscle of the foot propel the snail along in search of food. The flying gurnard or loloaʻu (right) is a lucky find for divers. The gurnard usually creeps along the bottom on its pelvic fins, stirring up the sand with little whisks (visible here near the fish's eyes) made up of its forward pectoral fin rays. In this way, small crustaceans, mollusks, and flounders are flushed from the sand, and then eaten. When the gurnard feels threatened it flares the large "wings," which make it appear much larger than it is, and thus less tempting to a predator. When really alarmed, a dorsal spine is raised on the head and the gurnard makes a loud popping sound. The belly of this female whitetip reef shark or manō-lālā-kea (left) is stretched and full of pups, and she is close to giving birth. A litter usually consists of five to seven pups, which receive no maternal care and must make their own way from the start. Whitetips generally mate in the summer and fall, giving birth in the spring and summer.

UNGIA SCUTARIA

MONTIPORA CAPITATA GROWING OVER PORITES COMPRESSA

PORITES COMPRESSA

BURROWS MADE BY ALPHEUS DEUTEROPUS; CORAL: MONTIPORA PATULA

ACANTHASTER PLANCI

Mushroom coral (top left) gets its name because the radial pattern of the septa resemble the "gills" of a mushroom cap. In this photo the tentacles are retracted, but at night the tentacles extend to capture plankton which is then passed to the mouth inside the central groove. Competition for space is no less vigorous among corals than among other reef inhabitants. Rice coral (top right) grows like a blanket around finger coral, and eventually the finger coral will be overtaken. Snapping shrimp burrows (above right) in the central coral garden are visible from quite a distance and sometimes resemble Hawaiian petroglyphs. The shrimps may use chemical and mechanical means to kill the coral, forming branching channels. Inside the channels the shrimps cultivate algae which they eat. Tiny white stinging hydroids, barely visible in this photo, may protect them from predators. Tiny flower-shaped polyps build the hard calcium skeleton of finger coral (above left). The tentacles of each polyp extend into the water to capture even tinier plankton, but not without risk. Shaved off by a fish, the tentacles of these coral polyps are regenerating, and in time, the injury will heal completely. The crown-of-thorns sea star (left) is a feeding machine. It extends its stomach outside its body over desirable species of corals, then secretes chemicals which dissolve the coral tissue, leaving a dead white coral skeleton. On a few summer nights every year, rice coral spawns (opposite). Influenced by the phase of the moon, each rice coral polyp produces eggs and sperm which are packaged in a bundle and then, when the moon is new, released at a precise time—a beautiful and unearthly sight. The buoyant eggs give the sperm a ride to the surface, where the bundle breaks apart and the eggs and sperm of different colonies mix.

The white-stripe urchin shrimp lives among the spines of the highly venomous, and rarely encountered, blue-spotted urchin. The spines and venomous nature of the urchin makes it almost predator-proof, and the shrimp is free to hop from spine to spine in safety.

SHRIMP: STEGOPONTONIA COMMENSALIS; URCHIN: ASTROPYGA RADIATA

The yellow-spotted snake eel is one of Molokini's most mysterious inhabitants. During the day these eels extend their heads above the sand, actively pumping water across their gills as if out of breath. When approached too closely they quickly withdraw beneath the sand, often digging backwards in a sinuous pattern visible from above, then emerging several feet from their original position.

CALLECHELYS LUTEA

CRAB: LYBIA EDMONDSONI; SEA ANEMONES: TRIACTIS PRODUCTA

In an amazing display of "tool use," Edmondson's boxing crab or kūmimi pua (above), holds an anemone in each claw, raising and waving them in a threatening manner at any danger. The crab, which spends most of its time living under rocks, induces the anemones to detach from the bottom, then uses their stinging capability for its own defense. Sea cucumber crabs (opposite, above) are usually found living inside the sea cucumber's mouth, although they can also be found on the body or even within the anus. This crab is hunkering down into the skin of the sea cucumber by pulling the skin up with its claws and by digging into the skin with the tips of its legs. The resemblance of the crab to the body of the sea cucumber, including the flecks of sand, is so perfect that when it sinks down into the skin of the cucumber it is virtually invisible. In case it is seen by a passing fish, large false eye spots on the back of the crab challenge the predator. Taking shelter behind empty helmet shell egg cases, the sand octopus (opposite, below) is the second most commonly seen octopus at Molokini. It typically seeks shelter under the sand, often clasping two old bivalve shells, and sandwiching itself between them. This species seems most active at night, although little is known of its life history and it has not yet been given a scientific name.

CRAB: LISSOCARCINUS ORBICULARIS; SEA CUCUMBER: HOLOTHURIA ATRA

OCTOPUS SP.

DASCYLLUS ALBISELLA

AULOSTOMUS CHINENSIS

Through the membrane of a trumpetfish's mouth (left) can be seen the scales of a Hawaiian Dascyllus, which this trumpetfish has just swallowed. The trumpetfish stalks its prey by hiding behind larger fishes, or hanging vertically in the water column where its small cross-section may not be seen as a threat. When a fish is near enough, the trumpetfish strikes, expanding its mouth and inhaling the fish head-first. Not all strikes are successful. This Hawaiian Dascyllus (above, top) has had a brush with death, (the predator is unknown) and is torn and bloody. Although the injury looks severe, this fish may survive. The Dascyllus caught by the trumpetfish did not, however, and a half hour later (above) appears as a lump in the trumpetfish's belly.

CRAB: TRAPEZIA TIGRINA; CORAL: POCILLOPORA MEANDRINA

Some of Molokini's moray eels have occupied their territories for more than twenty years (left). Yellowmargin morays or puhi paka, like this one, frequently extend from the reef during the day, perhaps to monitor the area for other yellowmargins. They are fiercely territorial and are sometimes seen with large cuts and injuries, presumably from such battles. At night they swim about in search of their prey fishes. The life of the red-spotted guard crab and the cauliflower coral (above) are closely intertwined. The guard crab defends the coral from predators, pinching at the tube feet of sea stars or extending a claw toward the snout of a butterflyfish. In return, the crab receives a safe haven in the deep maze of coral branches, and is even provided with food. Special lipids are concentrated in the tips of the coral's tentacles, specifically, it is thought, to attract and keep these beneficial crabs. The cost of regenerating its tentacle tips is greatly outweighed by the benefit of the crab's defense. This crab is a female, as can be seen from the mass of eggs tucked against her abdomen. The honor of fastest-strike-on-the-reef goes to the mantis shrimp (right), which captures its prey in as little as three milliseconds with praying mantis-like arms. This species is usually seen at the entrance to its burrow, waiting for fishes or crustaceans to enter the strike zone. The highly developed eyes send multiple images to the brain. When these merge into one crisp image, the prey is in the killing zone and the mantis shrimp strikes.

LYSIOSQUILLINA MACULATA

Appearing surreal in this closeup, the world to this tiny imperial shrimp is the body surface of a sea cucumber. The odd protrusions are the sea cucumber's tube feet. Note that this shrimp is a female with eggs, and the eyes of her offspring are already visible.

SHRIMP: PERICLIMENES IMPERATOR; SEA CUCUMBER: STICHOPUS SP.

FORCIPIGER FLAVISSIMUS

FORCIPIGER LONGIROSTRIS

FORCIPIGER LONGIROSTRIS

The long snout of the forcepsfish or lau-wiliwili-nukunuku-oiʻoi (above) can reach into tight places to pick at the tube feet of urchins, worms, fish eggs, and small crustaceans. It takes a good eye to tell this species apart from the longnose butterflyfish, unless the latter is in its less common, dark brown melanistic form (both at left). The longnose has a slightly longer snout than the forcepsfish, and has tiny black dots on the chest. The longnose butterflyfish was the first fish described from the Hawaiian Islands, having been collected during Captain James Cook's third voyage in the late 1770s. The diet of the longnose butterflyfish is not as varied as that of the forcepsfish, consisting mostly of small crustaceans. The female pinktail triggerfish or humuhumu-hiʻu-kole (below) aerates her eggs by flapping her pectoral fins. Together with the male (opposite) she chases away egg-eating predators— and divers! The eggs are laid at night, and because of their rapid development, need only be guarded for one day.

MELICHTHYS VIDUA (FEMALE)

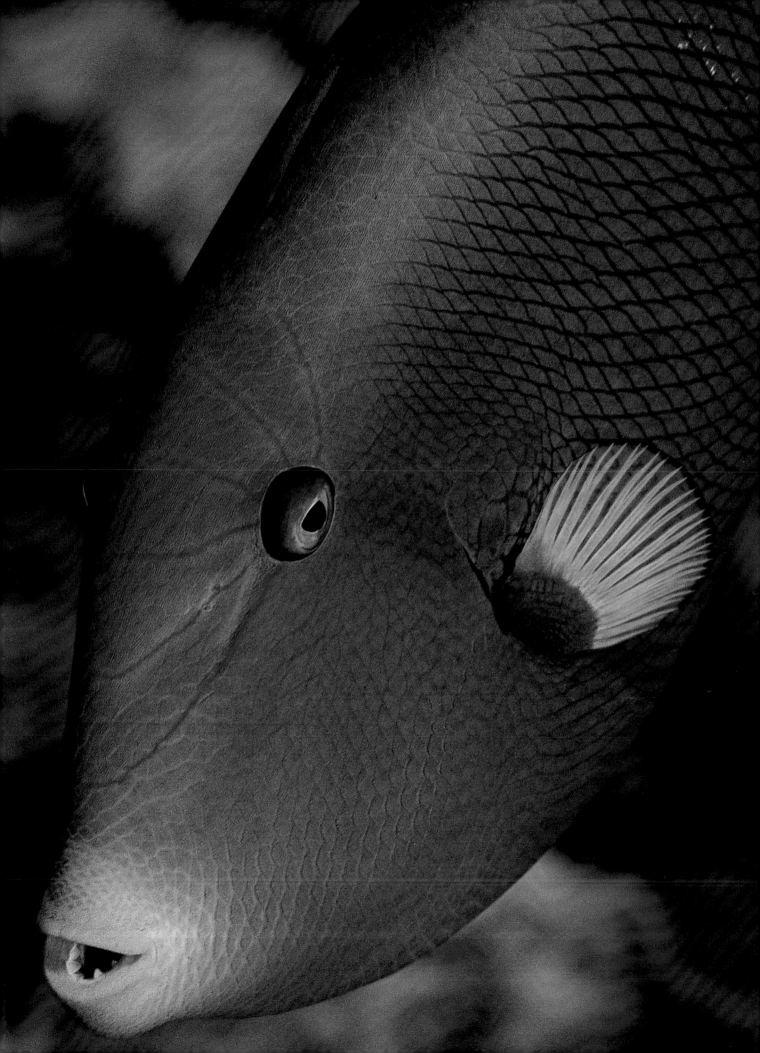

GORGASIA HAWAIIENSIS

Slender and shy, garden eels (above) extend from their burrows, gracefully picking plankton from the water column. Their large eyes allow them to see tiny plankton as well as predators, which is important since garden eels must expose so much of themselves during feeding. When danger nears in the form of a jack or a diver, the eels withdraw into their burrows, but waste no time emerging to feed once the danger has passed. Diving at night is the only way to see this beautiful snail (opposite, top) which lives buried beneath sand during the day. At night it emerges to roam the sand in search of crabs and shrimps. Just after this photo was taken the harp shell lunged forward and engulfed a hermit crab which had left the protection of its shell, possibly to make a quicker (but in this case ultimately unsuccessful) escape. In cutaways along the edge of the central coral garden, whitetip reef sharks or manō-lālā-kea (right) sometimes rest during the day. Young pups from the same litter spread out at night to feed but gather together in a hole by morning. As they mature they become more independent, eventually spending their days resting alone.

HARPA MAJOR

TRIAENODON OBESUS

XYRICHTYS PAVO

CORIS BALLIEUI (FEMALE)

XYRICHTYS PAVO

XYRICHTYS PAVO

CORIS BALLIEUI (MALE)

The female (above) and male (left) of this beautiful pastel wrasse were once thought to be separate species. Lined coris typically live in hundreds of feet of water, but sometimes individuals settle in shallow water at Molokini. When they do, they live along the edge of coral and sand. They feed during the day and burrow into the sand at night. Razorfishes or lae-nihi (far left) get their name from their narrow bodies and blade-like foreheads, which enable them to quickly dive into the sand when threatened. The juvenile peacock razorfish (bottom) looks very different from the adult (top). Small fish are more vulnerable to predators and therefore many small wrasses have evolved specialized disguises. The juvenile peacock razorfish resembles a drifting leaf. As it matures, the long dorsal spine becomes shorter and its color shifts to blend with the sand. The adult can also have a jet-black color phase (middle).

BOTHUS PANTHERINUS

The panther flounder or pāki'i (above) is one of many ambush predators which strike at small fishes and crustaceans that do not realize it is there. Flounders are unusual in that during transformation from a larval fish to a juvenile, one of their eyes migrates over the top of the head, resulting in both eyes being located on the same side of the body. This has allowed flounders to fill a unique niche—that of a fish that can hide flat against the bottom. The pearl fish (opposite, above) lives inside the respiratory tract of the sea cucumber; however the respiratory tract is not inside the mouth as one would expect. Instead, in an unusual biological twist, it is located in the anus, which is where the pearl fish finds shelter. Fire dartfish (right) are common in the western Pacific but are seen in Hawai'i only sporadically. Due to some unknown inhibiting factor, they do not usually breed successfully in Hawai'i, and therefore years might pass during which we do not see even one. Perhaps temperature or some other factor is not favorable here at the easternmost edge of their range.

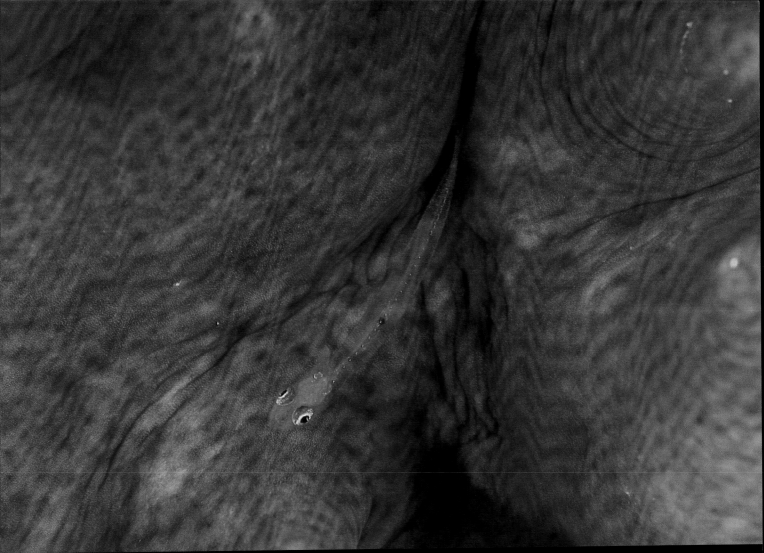

PEARL FISH: CARAPUS MOURLANI; SEA CUCUMBER: STICHOPUS SP.

NEMATELEOTRIS MAGNIFICA

POECILOCONGER FASCIATUS

Until 1989, only five specimens of the spotted conger eel (above) had ever been recorded in the world—one in Madagascar, one in Tahiti, one in Indonesia, and two in Hawai'i. They are difficult to spot during the day as they blend in well with the bottom, and withdraw into the sand as divers approach. At night they swim out in the open in search of small fishes. Thousands of pointed tube feet allow the magnificent sand star (opposite, below and middle) to travel and bury itself at impressive speeds. This species is Hawai'i's largest sea star, and the one with the most arms. It buries itself beneath the sand during the day, the only evidence of its presence being a faint depression in the sand, and even that is obscured by the shifting sand as morning wears on. It feeds on echinoderms such as heart urchins and sea stars, which it swallows whole! Powerful jaws and teeth allow the barred filefish or 'ō'ili (opposite, top) to eat hard corals as well as echinoderms and other hard invertebrates, and loud crunching can sometimes be heard when in their presence. They often turn upside-down for a better feeding position. At night, these and a few other species of filefishes have been observed resting on the bottom with their teeth clamped onto corals in a behavior called "mooring."

CANTHERHINES DUMERILII; CORAL: POCILLOPORA EYDOUXI

LUIDIA MAGNIFICA

LUIDIA MAGNIFICA

At night, squids, or mūheʻe, ascend from deep water to hunt, either alone or in groups like this one. Squids possess eight arms plus two tentacles. These two tentacles can be extended in a flash to capture fishes. The many suction cups hold the fish while it is being consumed.

SEPIOTEUTHIS LESSONIANA

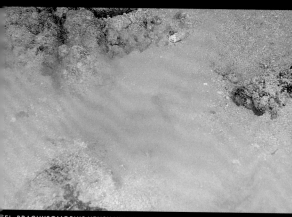

EEL: BRACHYSOMOPHIS HENSHAWI; TRIGGERFISH: MELICHTHYS VIDUA

Perhaps Molokini's most patient hunter, the Henshaw eel is usually almost invisible, with only the tip of its snout exposed above the sand. The remarkable sequence of photographs above documents the eel exploding from the sand to grab a triggerfish in its very powerful jaws. The eel then yanked the hapless triggerfish under the sand, and swallowed it whole. A different individual (right) is extended further than is typical from its burrow. Note the length of the jawline. Although in flash photography the eels can appear a bright red or pink, at depth these colors blend in with the sand and rubble.

Although more active at night, whitetip reef sharks, or manō-lālā-kea, are also seen during the day at Molokini, where they feed, mate, and give birth. Strangely, the species name "obesus" means swollen or fat, while you can see from the photograph that these sharks are actually quite slender.
TRIAENODON OBESUS

Inner Rim

Bathed in sunlight, the shallows tucked up against the inside of Molokini's curve are a rich mixture of corals, rock, and diverse marine life.

The inner rim of the crescent provides habitats distinctly different from the central reef area. Swells breaching the rim tumble and break corals and rocks, creating many places to hide and new substrate every time there is big storm surf. Algae grow on the newly available surfaces and a variety of corals take hold and begin new colonies. Fish life becomes more diverse having a larger variety of food items and shelters available. Periodically, surf from big storms completely rearranges the bottom, keeping the underwater community in flux and species diversity high. Just as fires on a prairie open up habitat for new plant species, storm waves produce the same results on the reef.

The hardiest coral inhabiting this rough-and-tumble area is cauliflower coral. Its small compact colonies possess stubby flattened branches not easily broken by surf. Living among the branches are pairs of shrimps and crabs, including several species of snapping shrimps. Using one enlarged claw, these shrimps produce click sounds which are powerful enough to stun small prey. The sound also defines their territories, keeping other snapping shrimps

The harlequin shrimp is one of the most exciting finds underwater. It frequently occupies branched corals during the day, often feeding on a sea star that it has captured and dragged back to the coral during its forays at night. The large paddle-shaped appendages are raised in a threatening manner when it perceives danger and can be discarded as a distraction when escaping.

out of their particular coral head and assuring an adequate food supply. The continual snapping of thousands of shrimps produces a light crackling sound (something like bacon frying), that surrounds the diver or snorkeler in shallow water along the rim of the crater.

Several times each spring cauliflower coral reproduces in a dramatic event known as coral spawning. At a precise time shortly after sunrise, heads of cauliflower coral begin releasing white clouds of sperm and eggs making the reef appear to be "smoking." In just five minutes, the crystal clear water can become so milky that snorkelers or divers cannot even see each other. By synchronizing the release of their eggs and sperm, the coral colonies maximize the chance of fertilization and the mixing of genetic material, thereby ensuring survival of their species.

The inner rim is the area most accessible to snorkelers. The water here is shallow and boats find it easy to moor. Although fish feeding has not been allowed for years, food in various forms is still occasionally introduced from boats, and many fishes linger near the surface waiting for the accidental morsel. In addition, these fishes are accustomed to the presence of people. Many can therefore be approached within arm's length, to be observed and photographed in the bright light near the surface.

Closer to the bottom is an array of sheltering sites supporting a large variety of fishes. Thousands of tiny damselfishes, dartfishes, angelfishes and wrasses, hover just inches above the substrate, diving into crevices when threatened. Moray eels of all

CHAETODON FREMBLII

The endemic Hawaiian flagtail (right) is a shallow water fish that schools during the day and chiefly feeds at night. Most endemic Hawaiian fishes have a known or surmised ancestor species somewhere else in the Pacific, but not the bluestripe butterflyfish or kīkākapu (left). Called a relic, its relatives no longer exist. The ancestor may not have adapted to meet changing conditions, but the bluestripe in Hawaiʻi did. Therefore, it still exists. All the stiff hairs protruding from the orange reef lobster (below) are giving it information about its surroundings. By day it hides in the reef with its large claws extended in defense. At night it emerges to scavenge for food.

ENOPLOMETOPUS OCCIDENTALIS

KUHLIA XENURA

sizes slither through small passages in search of hiding fishes which they are uniquely specialized to reach with their long flexible bodies. Octopuses excavate small dens, and the females wall themselves inside, laying their eggs and tending them for several weeks until they hatch. Large wrasses pick up rocks and toss them aside in search of small crabs, snails, and brittle stars which suddenly find themselves exposed. The nooks and crevices are infinite along the inner rim, housing millions of tiny animals.

Beginning in late morning, manta rays often arrive inside the rim, gliding into position over the territories of cleaner wrasses and other small fishes. Here they hover while the fishes pick off parasites and dead skin, sometimes plunging deep within the ray's gill slits to do so. A unique pattern of spots on the underside of each ray makes identifying individuals possible. Photos of the same ray taken years apart indicate that some of these blue-water feeders return repeatedly to the same cleaning areas inside Molokini.

Also living within the crater's rim are juvenile sharks. Sometimes an entire litter of newborn whitetip reef shark pups will gather by day to hide under a ledge, splitting up at night to feed. Other shark pups, the gray reef sharks, swim above the reefs during the day in a small group. At this stage they seem to prefer the protected waters of the inner rim to the more exposed outer walls. As they mature, they spread further and further apart, eventually, as adults, traveling alone. Many divers and snorkelers have seen their first shark at Molokini. Increasingly rare elsewhere, these long-lived creatures are fortunate to live in the relative protection of the sanctuary boundaries.

The usually calm, protected waters of Molokini's inner rim offer a surprising diversity of animal life. Large open-ocean fishes frequently enter the crater, usually for cleaning, and endangered Hawaiian monk seals occasionally stop for a few days to feed and haul out on the inner wave bench. Always different, the inner rim is in many ways Molokini's most interesting area.

STETHOJULIS BALTEATA

SCORPIONFISH: TAENIANOTUS TRIACANTHUS; ALGA: HALIMEDA SP.

Sacoglossans (left) such as this inch-long ornate Elysia are shell-less snails that are closely related to nudibranchs. Quietly grazing on algae, they are easily overlooked by divers as well as predators. Like so many wrasses this male belted wrasse or ʻōmaka (top) is much more colorful than his female counterpart. He began life as a dark-gray female, then changed sex into this vibrant male. This one has just swallowed a prey item, typically a worm, mollusk, or crustacean, and the debris picked up with it is being discarded through the gill openings. Although this species is found only in Hawaiʻi, a very similar-looking relative exists in other areas of the Pacific. The unique body shape of the leaf scorpionfish (above), and its habit of flopping occasionally from side to side, are thought to make it resemble a leaf or a piece of debris being moved by the surge. Both predator and prey may not realize that it is a living fish and the leaf scorpionfish can feed in safety. Although a member of the scorpionfish family, this is the only one in Hawaiʻi believed to lack venomous spines.

ELYSIA ORNATA

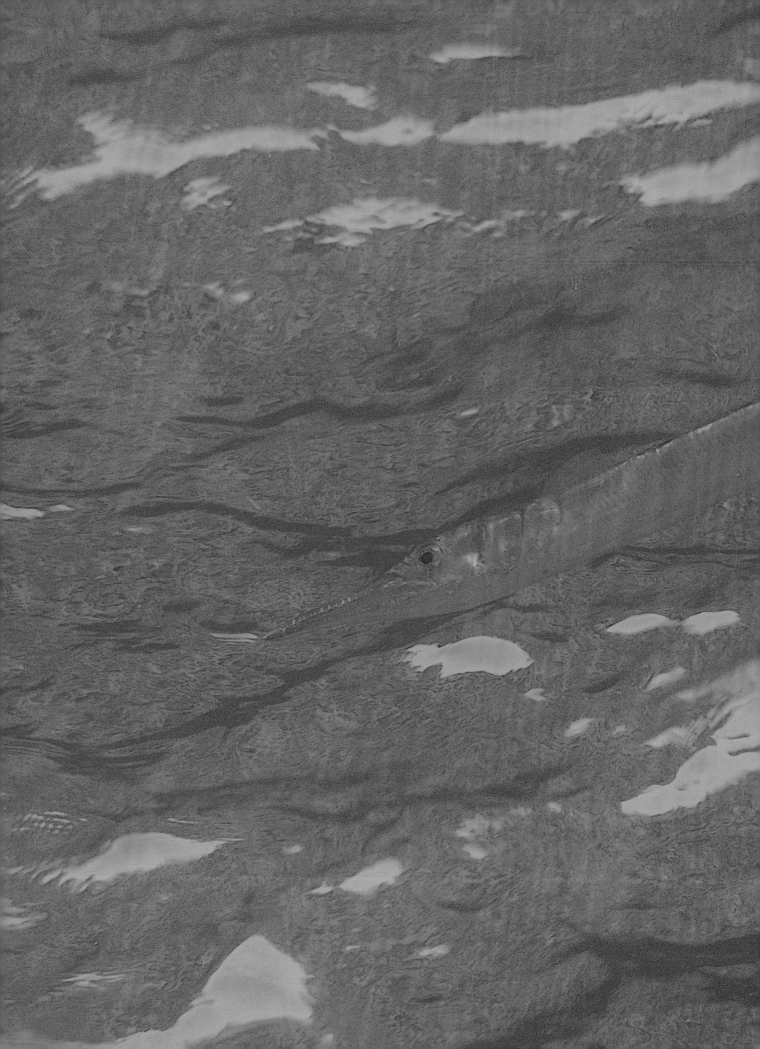

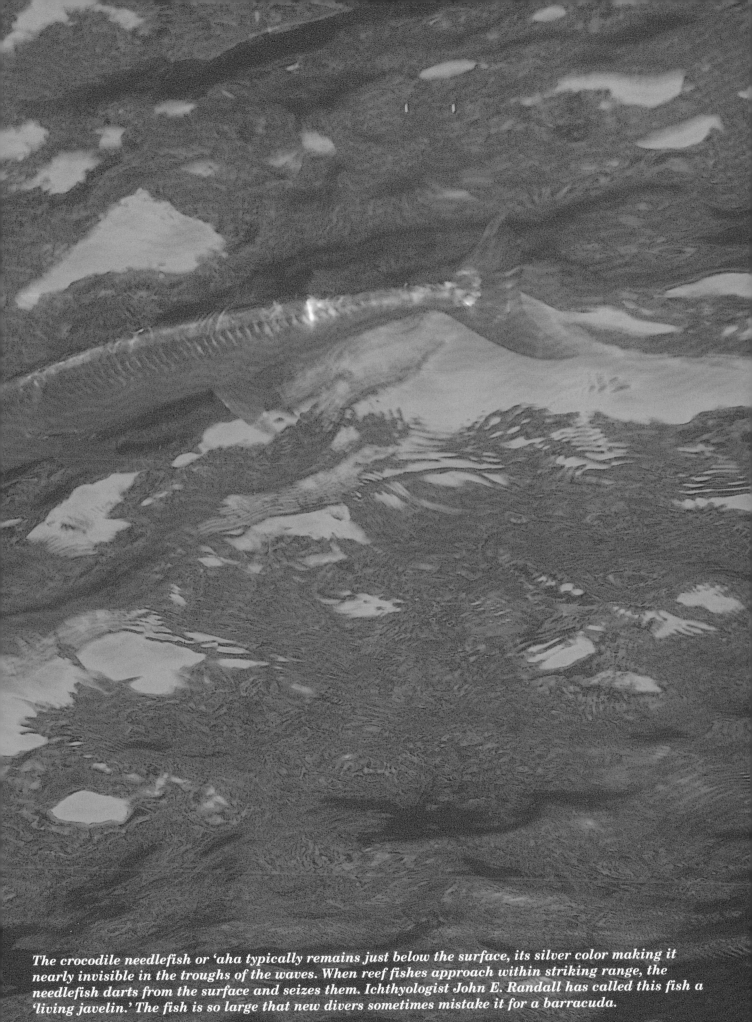

The crocodile needlefish or 'aha typically remains just below the surface, its silver color making it nearly invisible in the troughs of the waves. When reef fishes approach within striking range, the needlefish darts from the surface and seizes them. Ichthyologist John E. Randall has called this fish a 'living javelin.' The fish is so large that new divers sometimes mistake it for a barracuda.

TYLOSURUS CROCODILUS

EXALLIAS BREVIS

This colorful male shortbodied blenny or pāoʻo kauila (above) is guarding and aerating eggs. He may have several clutches of eggs, laid by one or more females, under his care at one time, all different colors. The yellow eggs are recently laid, still containing a lot of yolk. The silver eggs behind the blenny are about five days old, the silver color due to the pigment in the eyes of the larvae. They will hatch in a few more days. Only about three inches long, the Hawaiian whitespotted toby (opposite, above) catches the eye of more divers and snorkelers than most species, thanks to its striking polka-dot pattern and the fact that they are very common. Swimming very close to the bottom, often in pairs, they peck at sponges and algae. In doing so, they risk being grabbed by sand-dwelling predators such as octopus and mantis shrimps. One lucky little toby was attacked by such a predator, but puffed up so big that the predator could not pull it into its hole. It was released as we approached and the puffer swam safely away. Yellow tangs or lau-ī-pala (opposite) are among the most striking on the reef, especially when congregated in numbers. The characteristic surgeonfish blade is accented with white for increased visibility as a warning to predators. At night, this fish turns a very dull yellow, perhaps to become less conspicuous to predators with good night vision.

CANTHIGASTER JACTATOR

ZEBRASOMA FLAVESCENS

At night, many parrotfishes rest on the bottom and secrete a mucus "cocoon" around themselves for protection (below). Moray eels and sharks, hunting in the darkness by following the scent of sleeping fishes, may not detect the parrotfish whose scent is blocked by the mucus. In the morning, the parrotfish emerges from the cocoon which falls apart or is pecked apart by other fishes. Turtles are rarely seen at Molokini due to the lack of shelter and macro-algae on which the common green sea turtle feeds. This hawksbill turtle or honu 'ea (opposite), which feeds on sponges, remained at Molokini for a few months, apparently finding acceptable foraging habitat. This pair of redlip parrotfish or uhu pālukaluka (opposite, below) follows the general parrotfish color scheme—the male (bottom) is bright blue and green, and the female is ruddy brown. They are some of the largest fishes on the reef and travel within large territories scraping algae from rocks and dead corals. It is easy to see in this photo that their "beaks" are made of many teeth fused together. Coralline algae has been scraped from the rock in front of the male redlip parrotfish.

CHLORURUS SORDIDUS

ERETMOCHELYS IMBRICATA

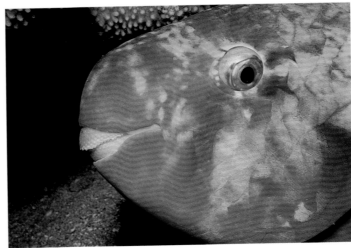

SCARUS RUBROVIOLACEUS (FEMALE)

SCARUS RUBROVIOLACEUS (MALE)

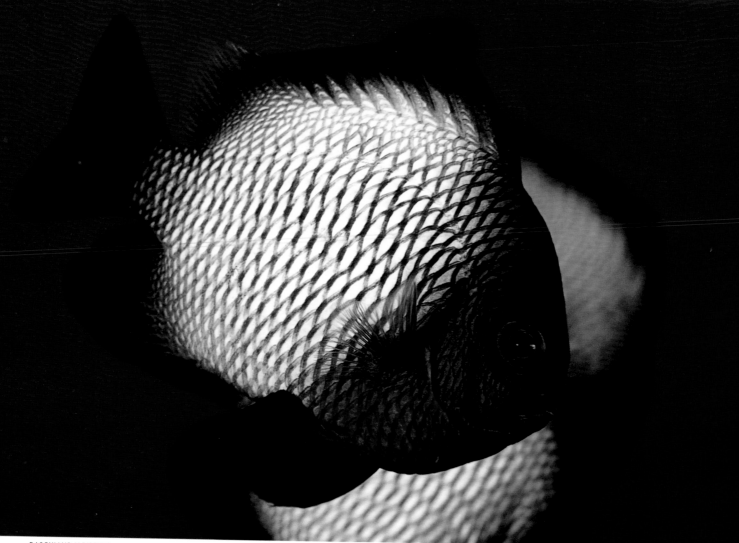

DASCYLLUS ALBISELLA

Male Hawaiian Dascyllus or ʻāloʻiloʻi (above) stake out a territory on the reef and live there for life. At certain times he (as well as many of the other male Hawaiian Dascyllus on the reef) will court females by swooping and fluttering over his territory, attempting to entice one to lay her eggs on a rock in his space. As she does, he follows closely behind fertilizing them (right). She then leaves and he remains to defend them from predators for several days until they hatch. Some males are quite pugnacious and will even bite divers who get too close. This feathery crown of tentacles (opposite, above), captures food and performs the task of respiration for the feather duster worm. Particles caught in the hairy tentacles are then transported by cilia along a groove to the mouth. Since these worms typically inhabit turbid water where suspended particles are more highly concentrated, they are rarely seen in Molokini's clear waters. When a threat is detected, the crown is withdrawn in a snap. The large, brilliant orange spot on the body of the achilles tang or pākuʻikuʻi (opposite) accents the sharp blade near the tail, warning predators of its painful defense. Surgeonfishes graze on algae with their faces close to the bottom, and such a defense at the opposite end of the body is quite useful.

DASCYLLUS ALBISELLA

SABELLASTARTE SPECTABILIS

ACANTHURUS ACHILLES

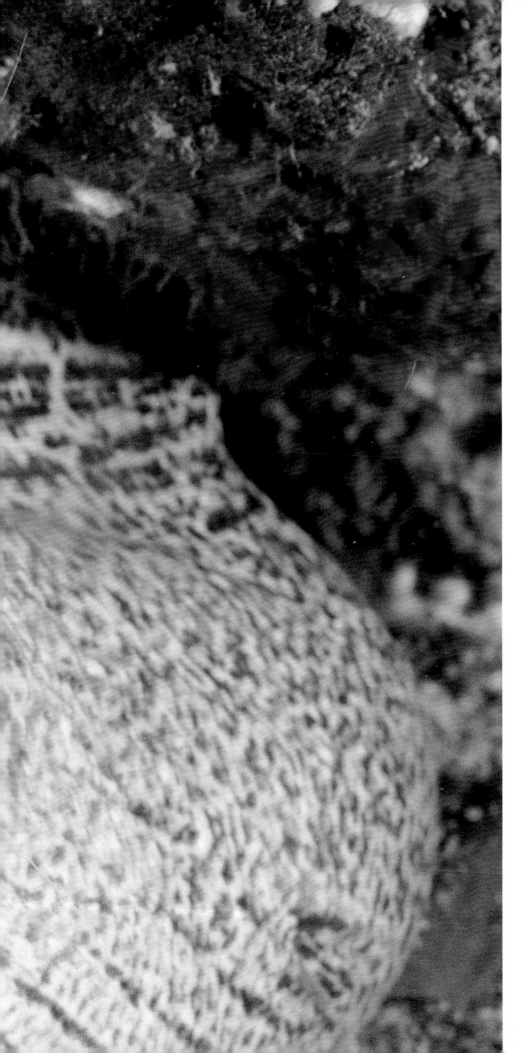

An amazing and seemingly unlikely relationship exists between cleaner shrimps and the eels they clean. Through evolution, those eels which did not eat the shrimps but allowed them to clean inside their mouths, apparently derived some benefit not received by eels that did not allow cleaning. The cooperative eels were more successful in passing on their genes and now eels regularly engage in this activity.

The shrimps that risked their lives by exposing themselves to fishes and eels obtained a valuable food source and gained some advantage over shrimps that did not utilize this source of food.

Shrimps that are cleaners often have long white antennae that they extend from a place of shelter to advertise their presence so fishes and eels will approach. In this way they do not have to expose their entire bodies to predators that are not on their list of potential cleaning subjects, such as octopus, jacks, or scorpionfishes.

When the fish or eel approaches, the shrimp may clean the outer body surface or reach tiny pinchers inside gill openings and the mouth. The shrimps are careful to leave some of their legs on the outside, however, in case a quick exit becomes necessary. When the eel has had enough, it gives its head a quick shake and the shrimp darts out.

MORAY: GYMNOTHORAX UNDULATUS
SHRIMP: LYSMATA AMBOINENSIS

THALASSOMA TRILOBATUM

The surge zone is the favored habitat of the Christmas wrasse or ʻāwela (above) which is likely to be seen by snorkelers due to its shallow habitat. While its body shape and coloration resemble those of the closely related parrotfishes, it does not have the parrotfish "beak." Instead it has powerful jaws that can crush crabs and mollusks. Perhaps the most striking fish on the reef when illuminated is the flame angelfish (opposite, above). This species is so uncommon that only a handful are ever in residence at Molokini at any given time. They live close to the bottom and graze on algae. A distinguishing characteristic of all angelfishes is the prominent spine extending from the gill plate. The stunning and famous moorish idol or kihikihi (opposite) is a quiet resident, poking its elongate snout into crevices to feed mostly on sponges. It is the only member of its family and is actually related to surgeonfishes.

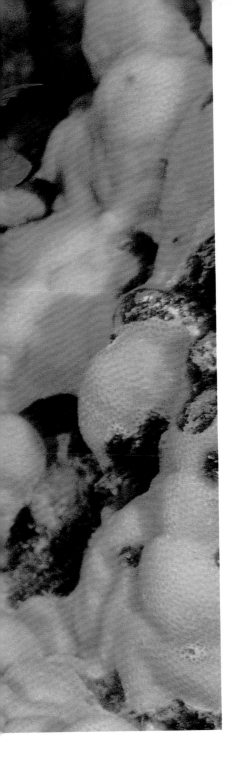

CENTROPYGE LORICULA

ZANCLUS CORNUTUS

POCILLOPORA MEANDRINA

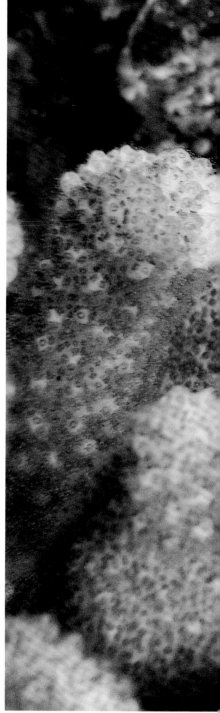

PSEUDOCHEILINUS TETRATAENIA

POCILLOPORA MEANDRINA

As the above photo suggests, the fourline wrasse is very shy, and spends little time exposed. At only about two-and-one-half inches, remaining among crevices and corals is its best defense. A few times in the spring, these cauliflower corals (left) release their eggs and sperm in synchrony, so that chances of cross-fertilization are maximized. When the exact moment arrives, each coral head begins releasing its eggs and sperm which are so tiny that the entire crater rim appears to be "smoking" (left, above).

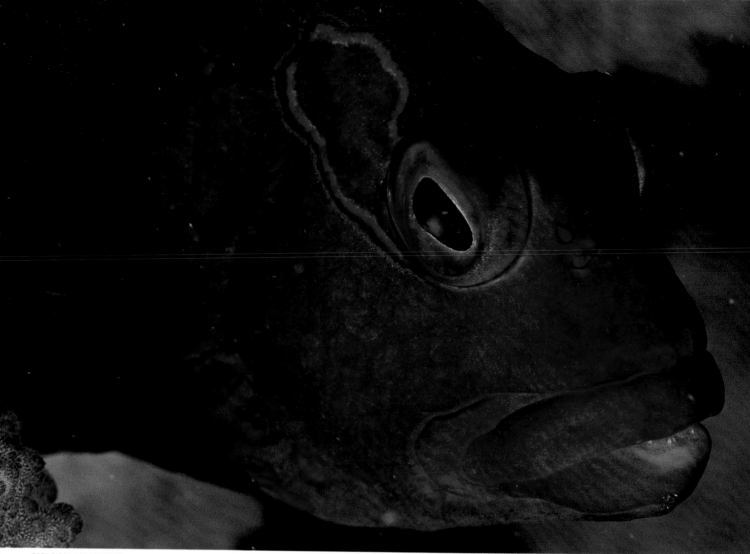

PARACIRRHITES ARCATUS

*This closeup (above) makes it obvious how
the arc-eye hawkfish or pilikoʻa got its name.
Since it perches on corals or rocks, it is easy
for divers to spot as it scans the water for
small planktonic animals which drift past.
If a diver gets too close, the hawkfish picks
itself up, swims a short distance and sets
down again on fins specialized for perching.
The cornetfish or nūnū peke (opposite, top) is
a relative of the trumpetfish and pipefishes,
as can be seen from the structure of its
mouth. Like something from a Saturday
morning cartoon, this fish is so absurdly
thin that it can hide right out in the open.
Little Potter's angelfish (opposite, below) is
found only in Hawaiʻi, and it is our most
common angelfish. Males maintain harems,
so these fish are usually seen in small
groups. Like other members of the
surgeonfish family, the bluespine unicornfish
or kala (right) possesses defensive spines
near the tail. The spines are highlighted by
a blue warning color.*

NASO UNICORNIS

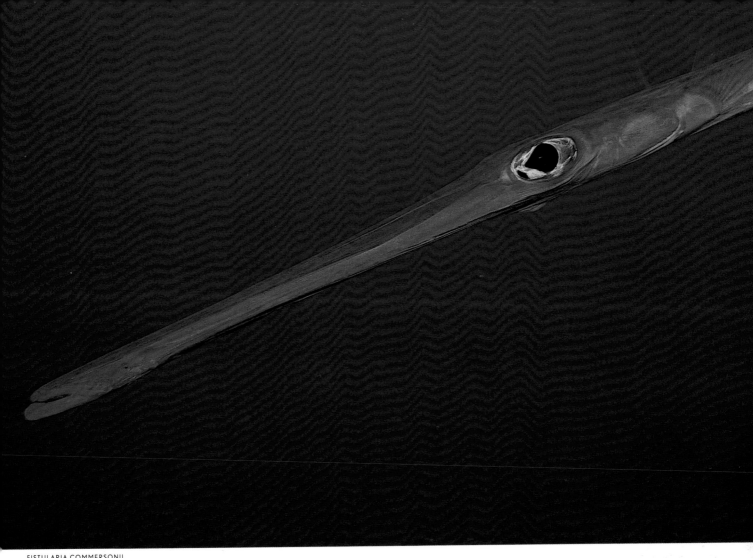

FISTULARIA COMMERSONII

CENTROPYGE POTTERI

These two male stareye parrotfish or pōnuhunuhu are engaging in a territorial dispute, while still keeping an eye on the photographer. Since a male parrotfish maintains a harem of females with which he alone spawns, this is not just a challenge over territory, but a challenge for the females within it.

CALOTOMUS CAROLINUS

LACTORIA DIAPHANA

Like a hovercraft, the spiny cowfish (above) suspends itself by sculling just above the bottom, using its tail as a rudder to steer. Well defended by their bony armor and spines, they pick at sponges and other sessile invertebrates spotted from their controlled hover. Moray eels or puhi are always long and slender, but the Okinawan moray (opposite, above) and the tiger moray (left) appear almost worm-like. That is because unlike most morays they do not have a noticeable dorsal fin. This allows them to get into even smaller spaces and reach small fishes that other eels cannot. Since they do little swimming, the dorsal fin is unnecessary. The complexity of the snail within the shell of the leviathan cowrie or leho pāuhu (right) is apparent in this photo. Appearing almost intelligent, the eyes are actually just light sensitive organs. The long tentacles detect its sponge prey and the hairy projections on the mantle increase the surface area for respiration.

SCUTICARIA TIGRINA

SCUTICARIA OKINAWAE

CYPRAEA LEVIATHAN

GOATFISH: PARUPENEUS MULTIFASCIATUS; BUTTERFLYFISH: CHAETODON LUNULA

The excitement created by so many raccoon butterflyfish has attracted this manybar goatfish or moano (above). It feeds on crustaceans, and perhaps some were flushed from hiding during all the activity. The two barbels under the chin can detect chemicals and are used to locate prey. This leatherback or lai, a type of jack, is being cleaned of mucus and parasites by a Hawaiian cleaner wrasse (opposite, above). It lives a mostly solitary life cruising the edge of the reef for fishes and crustaceans. Two venomous anal spines, visible on the underside of the leatherback, are one means of defense. The redbarred hawkfish or pili-koʻa (right), like others of its kind, has the habit of perching on corals or other elevated posts and swooping down on small animals—hence the name "hawkfish." They do not possess a swim bladder (which renders them heavier than water), and therefore spend most of their time perched. The lack of a swim bladder may allow them to swoop down on their prey with added momentum. This redbarred hawkfish is perched on the uncommon Duerden's coral, which resembles thick, ivory-colored lobes.

LEATHERBACK: SCOMBEROIDES LYSAN; WRASSE: LABROIDES PHTHIROPHAGUS

HAWKFISH: CIRRHITOPS FASCIATUS; CORAL: PAVONA DUERDENI

OCTOPUS CYANEA

OCTOPUS CYANEA (JUVENILE)

OCTOPUS CYANEA (SAME INDIVIDUAL AS ABOVE)

OCTOPUS CYANEA (EGGS)

This day octopus or he'e mauli (above) is a newly hatched juvenile. The day octopus lives only about a year, at which time the female selects a hole into which she crawls and barricades herself. There she lays her eggs in strands attached to the ceiling and guards and aerates them during the three weeks or so that they develop. The egg cases are clear and the developing octopuses can be seen within (left). Upon hatching, she unblocks the hole and, in the process of aerating, "blows" the tiny octopuses out into open water where they will develop over a period of weeks before settling to the bottom. During this time she does not eat, because if she left the hole, fishes would slip in and eat the eggs. After the eggs hatch, the female dies within days. The male also dies at about a year of age. Octopuses possess the impressive ability to change color and pattern in the blink of an eye. The two photos opposite, at top, show a day octopus one minute and how it had changed a split-second later. Octopuses are abundant but have so mastered the art of camouflage that they are not as frequently seen as might be expected.

TRITON SHELL: CHARONIA TRITONIS; SEA STAR: CULCITA NOVAEGUINEAE

The triton's trumpet snail (left) is a voracious predator. When the scent of a cushion star is detected, the triton will crawl toward it and capture the star by wrapping its large foot around it. A long, tubular proboscis extends from between the striped tentacles. It dissolves a hole through the skeleton of the star to get at the animal inside. It then narcotizes the star so that it stops moving and the triton can feed. The juvenile rockmover wrasse (right, at top) resembles a scrap of seaweed, and to complete the disguise, swims listlessly near the bottom as if it is drifting in the surge. Some predatory fishes may not even realize it is a fish. As it grows larger, it has fewer predators, and no longer needs the disguise. As an adult, the only remaining juvenile feature is the star pattern around the eye.

Look at the dorsal fin of the decoy scorpionfish (center right) and what do you see? Other fishes see a small fish hovering above the bottom, and when they approach to eat it, the decoy scorpion eats them! The little decoy, separated from the real fish by a transparent membrane, has a blue eye, a mouth, and a high dorsal spine. To make this lure even more appealing, the scorpionfish waves its decoy fin so that the "fish" appears to swim. The Hawaiian lionfish or nohu (below) also waves its dorsal fin, but in this case at threats—including the photographer. This fin has stiff spines that can inflict venomous puncture wounds. Usually inactive by day, the lionfish emerges in the evening and at night to feed. The pectoral fins resemble large fans which it spreads as a potential warning or when cornering prey.

NOVACULICHTHYS TAENIOURUS

IRACUNDUS SIGNIFER

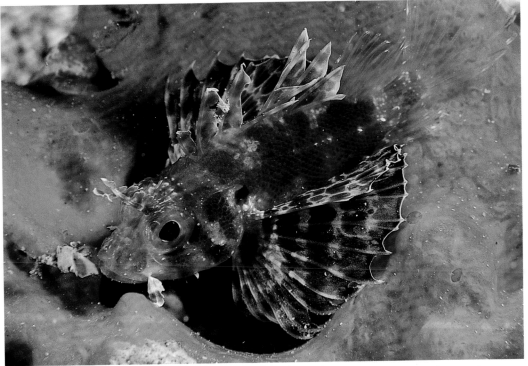

DENDROCHIRUS BARBERI

Spectacular coloration and large flared fins are part of the male flame wrasse's display as he chases other males away from his harem and keeps the females close-by. All this pays off in the end as he alone will spawn with the females. This species is found only in Hawai'i.
CIRRHILABRUS JORDANI

CHAETODON MILIARIS

PLAGIOTREMUS EWAENSIS

PTERELEOTRIS HETEROPTERA

SCORPAENOPSIS DIABOLUS

The milletseed butterflyfish or lau-wiliwili-nukunuku-ʻoiʻoi (above left) is one of the most common fish on the Hawaiian reef. They gather in great yellow clouds to pick planton.The devil scorpionfish or nohu ʻomakaha (above) is nearly impossible to see. Fleshy branching skin flaps break up its outline, its skin takes on the color of surrounding algae-covered rocks, and even the pupil of the eye is broken up by a strange branching shape. This last may serve to shield the eyes from harmful sun rays, a meaningful consideration for a fish which spends its time looking up from the bottom. Fishes and crustaceans that do not realize the scorpionfish is there are eaten. If the scorpionfish itself is threatened by a larger fish, it flares its pectoral fins, which are brilliant orange and yellow underneath—a warning that it is venomous. The spottail dartfish (near left) is a common inhabitant of the inner rim. They are found in pairs, picking plankton from the water while remaining within a safe distance of their burrow. When a threatening fish approaches, such as a snapper or a jack, they will dart to safety with amazing speed and coordination. The ʻEwa fangblenny (far left) is known for darting out from the reef and ripping mucus and tissue from other fishes. However, the fangblenny does this with small front teeth, not with the large "fangs," which are used for territorial and self-defense. Often the victim turns on the blenny and chases it back to the reef, where the blenny quickly backs into a perfectly sized hole in the rock, usually an empty worm snail shell.

ECHIDNA NEBULOSA

The snowflake moray or puhi-kāpā (above) is one of the few morays with a colorful pattern. Its long slender body can slither into tight places and reach small crabs and fishes, which it crushes with stout conical teeth. It is one of the eels occasionally seen traveling in the open during the day. The tuberculated frogfish (above right) is variable in color, as this photograph shows. No bigger than a ping pong ball, these tiny fishes secrete themselves among coral branches or in small holes. They fish for even smaller fishes and crustaceans using their worm-like lure which can be seen as an orange stem leaning against their forehead. When actively "fishing", the lure is held away from the forehead and moved in an enticing manner. When prey nears, the frogfish strikes with lightning speed. The juvenile stage of the yellowtail wrasse or hīnālea ʻakilolo (opposite, at center) looks nothing like the adult (bottom). Like many wrasses, the adult yellowtails keep territories which provide their food, and they prevent others of their species from feeding in that territory. Since the juveniles do not resemble the adult yellowtails, they are not perceived as a threat and are not chased off, allowing them a place to feed until they are big enough to defend their own territories. At that time their color pattern will change, beginning at the tail and advancing toward the head.

ANTENNATUS TUBEROSUS

CORIS GAIMARD (JUVENILE)

CORIS GAIMARD

OSTRACION WHITLEYI (FEMALE)

OSTRACION WHITLEYI (MALE)

Feeding together at right are a male and female psychedelic wrasse. The male, with his shockingly colored head, maintains a harem of females within a territory, and keeps other male psychedelic wrasses from entering. If he dies or is eaten, the dominant female in the harem begins to change color and sex to take his place. The slate blue male Whitley's trunkfish or moa (above) is a rare sight, but more likely to be seen at Molokini than off of Maui. The female (left), with her belly of yellow spots, demonstrates in this photo their habit of picking at algae and other organisms that live attached to the bottom. Strangely, the male and female are almost never seen together. The trunkfishes possess a bony case from which extend their fins, mouth and gill openings. With a black bar disguising its eye, and a false eye-spot near the tail, the threadfin butterflyfish (below) may confuse predators as to which end is which. If that doesn't work, the hypnotic chevron pattern on its body might.

CHAETODON AURIGA

ANAMPSES CHRYSOCEPHALUS (MALE AT LEFT)

The second most commonly seen shark at Molokini (after the whitetip reef shark) is the gray reef shark, although you are more likely to see them in deep water, as shown here. Somewhat beefier than the whitetip, the gray reef shark must swim constantly in order to breathe, while the whitetip can rest on the bottom. During certain times of year, grays gather for mating, and sometimes groups of ten or more—like these spunky juveniles—are observed.

CARCHARHINUS AMBLYRHYNCHOS

Outer Wall

Exposed to the open ocean, Molokini's outer slopes, rock ledges, and steep drop-offs are stark and dramatic against the deep blue.

A diver swimming from the inner rim over the crest and down the outer slope of the cone will note that the bottom falls away to great depths—gradually near the front end of the crater and more steeply as one nears the back. In places it becomes a vertical drop. This dramatic, jagged wall is a sight in itself, and the animal life that clings to it is exciting as well.

Exposed to frequent currents carrying abundant plankton, fishes work the water column near the wall, while still able to dart to safety in crevices if a jack or shark threatens. Hundreds of pyramid butterflyfish, rarer Thompson's butterflyfish, pennant butterflyfish, and sleek unicornfish hang in loose schools next to the wall, picking tiny organisms from the water. Larger plankton-feeders, such as manta rays, glide by. Their dark gray backs blend with the dark water, making them difficult to see from above. Large, hitch-hiking fish, called remoras, may attach themselves to the ray, taking advantage of the free ride to new food sources. But if the ray nears the reef, the remoras are in danger of being eaten by an improbable cleaner, the jack, which rips the remoras apart piece by piece as they cling to their host. Occasionally, the largest

plankton-feeder of all, the docile whale shark, approaches Molokini for a closer look.

Mating and spawning occur in the water column as well. Some fishes, such as the sleek unicornfish, gather by the hundreds around the time of the full moon, forming massive columns in the blue water along the wall. Males in courtship flash bright blue stripes on their faces, and raise their fins for added excitement.

After courtship, males and females of most fish species release their eggs and sperm into the sea, their parental duties finished. Females of some, however, lay their eggs on the vertical and horizontal rock surfaces within a male's territory, or in the case of triggerfishes, build nests in the sand on any available horizontal space. When another fish (or diver) approaches the eggs too closely, the male or female (or both) will drive the offender away leaving no doubt as to where the sometimes transparent eggs are laid.

These plankton-feeders require cleaning, as do the fishes within the crater, and periodically approach the wall to be cleaned by cleaner wrasses and other small fishes. More likely to be infested with parasites than fishes that live on the reef, they are preferred by the cleaners and are attended to immediately when they approach the cleaning station.

Many organisms live their lives anchored to the wall itself, ideally situated to receive a rich supply of food brought to it by flowing currents. The undersides of ledges and sections of the wall that remain shaded for all

Known from only five specimens, Pauline's Hypselodoris has so far been seen only in the Hawaiian Islands. Like other Hypselodoris it probably feeds on sponges. The brilliant coloration advertises to fishes that it is toxic, explaining why it can remain in the open during the day.

The bandit angelfish (right) is uncommon, and usually found deeper than one hundred feet. They often travel in pairs, roaming their large territory to feed on sponges. Oddly, the bandit angelfish—endemic to Hawai'i—has no close Indo-Pacific relative. Whale sharks (below) appear at Molokini at least several times a year, sometimes staying for hours or even a second day. These gentle sharks remain close to the surface, often allowing snorkelers and divers to come close. The backside of Molokini (left) is a dramatic wall facing blue water. Anything can pass by here.

RHINCODON TYPUS

DESMOHOLACANTHUS ARCUATUS

or part of the day are particularly rich, providing habitat for animals that do not need sunlight to survive. Most conspicuous are colonies of orange cup coral, which extend their tentacles to capture plankton, mostly at night or when a current is running. Black coral trees also grow in dark areas, branching far out into the water to feed where other corals cannot reach. The black corals provide habitat for other animals such as long-nose hawkfish, tiny gobies, and winged oysters. Stick-shaped trumpetfish can sometimes be seen hiding among the branches, waiting to dart out and nab small fishes that swim near.

Other predatory fishes, such as frogfishes, blend in so well with the surrounding habitat that other fishes do not realize the danger until it is too late. Molokini's outer rim is covered in many places with red encrusting sponge, and some of the frogfishes here assume a velvety red coloration not usually encountered elsewhere. The tiny juveniles, by contrast, are often a conspicuous bright yellow, resembling toxic yellow sponges.

The outer wall is a great place to encounter deep-dwelling fishes such as the yellow basslet, the blue-lined triggerfish, the red-tailed triggerfish, and the masked angelfish. All occasionally appear here within recreational diving depths, giving divers a rare opportunity to see and photograph these animals in shallow water.

Even rarer are visits by humpback whales which appear mysteriously and unpredictably from the blue. While encounters are usually limited to less than a minute, the memory created lasts a lifetime.

Although whales are seldom seen, their haunting songs seem to emanate from the blue depths and bounce off the wall, sometimes so loudly that one's chest cavity vibrates in resonance.

At the interface of volcanic wall and pelagic sea, the outer rim of Molokini is a breathtaking sight. Suspended above the abyss in ultra-clear water, divers swim between a dark cliff and a huge expanse of blue. Anything could swim by! Molokini's outer wall is Hawaiian diving at its most dramatic.

CHAETODON TINKERI

The outer wall provides excellent habitat for black coral (left), as frequent currents flow by bearing food. After decades of exposure to every conceivable reef inhabitant, parts of this black coral colony have been overgrown by red sponge, white soft coral, feathery hydroids, and other organisms. A rose-colored frogfish even perches among the branches. At depth, few of these colors are visible and the frogfish becomes almost invisible. It is rare to see a Tinker's butterflyfish (above) because of their preference for deep water, but when encountered they are curious and approach quite closely. Once believed to be endemic to Hawai'i, they have now been found at a few other central Pacific islands as well. These commensal gobies (right) live on black corals, gorgonians, or in this case, sponges. Pairs of the little gobies remain on the host day and night, even laying their eggs on a section of the host animal they have specially prepared. Should a predator threaten to pluck off the gobies, they scoot to the other side of their home, going round and round endlessly until the predator gives up.

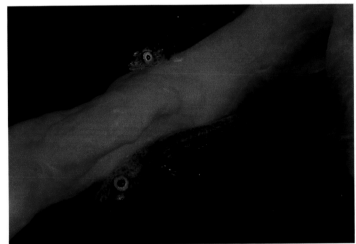

BRYANINOPS YONGEI

SQUIRRELFISH: SARGOCENTRON SPINIFERUM; SOLDIERFISH: MYRIPRISTIS KUNTEE

SARGOCENTRON ENSIFERUM

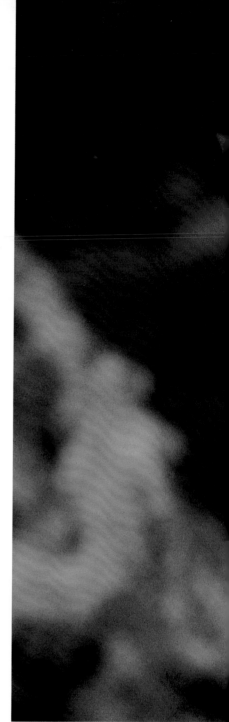

MYRIPRISTIS KUNTEE

MYRIPRISTIS CHRYSERES

The bulbous eyes and blunt snout of the epaulette soldierfish (above) enable this noctournal predator to focus on and capture large plankton, such as crab larvae, in the water at night. Yellow is one of the last colors visible at depth, thus the fins of the yellowfin soldierfish (bottom left) appear quite brilliant under ledges and in cracks below sixty feet during the day. Like iridescent rows of corn, the yellow stripes on the yellowstriped squirrelfish (middle left) stand out at depth. As the large eyes suggest, this is a nocturnal predator, feeding on bottom-dwelling crustaceans. Fishes which feed at night are generally larger and more spiny than fishes which hunt by day, as they are not able to dart for cover as easily as fishes which can see their escape route. Although both are red in color and have large eyes, squirrelfishes or ʻalaʻihi can be easily distinguished from soldierfishes or ʻūʻū by the spine extending from the squirrelfish gill plate. The spine, venomous and easy to spot on this large saber squirrelfish (top left), is lacking on the epaulette soldierfish behind it. At night all of these fishes emerge to hunt, the saber squirrelfish returning to the same shelter site every morning before sunrise.

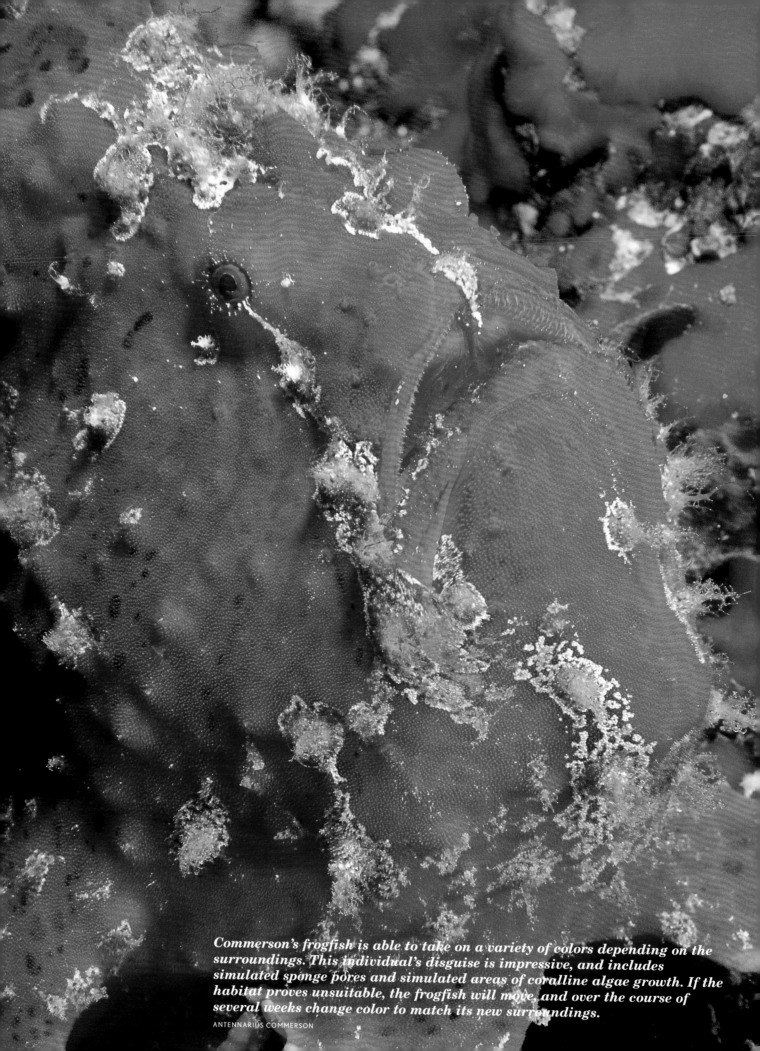

Commerson's frogfish is able to take on a variety of colors depending on the surroundings. This individual's disguise is impressive, and includes simulated sponge pores and simulated areas of coralline algae growth. If the habitat proves unsuitable, the frogfish will move, and over the course of several weeks change color to match its new surroundings.

ANTENNARIUS COMMERSON

,This frenetic scene occurs along the outer wall daily as thousands of mackerel scad or ʻōpelu capture plankton while still managing to remain in a school. When other jacks, such as amberjack, go after them, they cease feeding, school more tightly, and flee. A large school takes almost a minute to pass by from beginning to end.

DECAPTERUS MACARELLUS

XANTHICHTHYS MENTO (FEMALE)

Molokini is home to several rarely-seen species of triggerfishes that are variations of the same bold theme. All three of the species shown here hover above the bottom during the day feeding on plankton. The shallowest-dwelling and most numerous of these is the gilded triggerfish (bottom right), the more colorful male being pictured here. A little deeper is found the crosshatch triggerfish (female above, male top right). Deeper yet are the blue-lined triggerfish (center right) for which there is no known difference between the colors or patterns of the sexes. The blue-lined triggerfish are known to inhabit 200–600 foot waters, so it is quite a surprise to see them within recreational diving depths at Molokini.

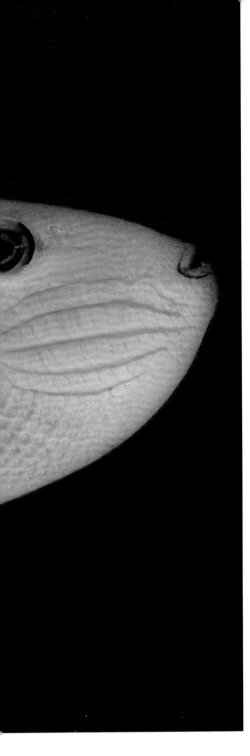

XANTHICHTHYS MENTO (MALE)

XANTHICHTHYS CAERULEOLINEATUS

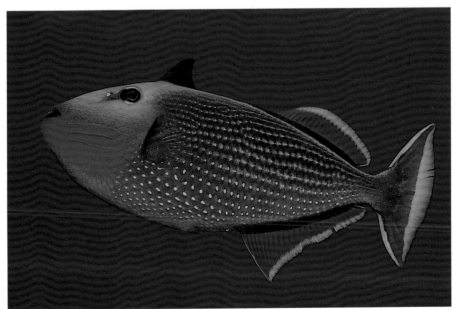

XANTHICHTHYS AUROMARGINATUS (MALE)

The yellow hairy hermit crab (opposite) is the largest (and hairiest!) hermit crab likely to be encountered by divers. It is so large it has few choices of shells when adult, being limited to a triton's trumpet or a partridge tun shell as here. Fisher's seahorse (right) is one of the most mysterious of the seahorses, and only a few specimens have ever been found—in Hawai'i, possibly (the specimens are in very poor condition) New Caledonia and Lord Howe Island (one specimen). The seahorse pictured here, about three inches long, was found at the ocean surface, drifting among floating debris. The pebble-like teeth of the zebra moray (below) tell us that this species feeds by crushing its prey, in this case mostly crabs but also urchins, hard-shelled snails, and even cowries. The dwarf moray (below right) is frequently found with sea urchins, probably because their spines offer protection for such a small eel. This species is often assumed to be a baby of one of the larger eels, because it doesn't get much bigger around than a pencil.

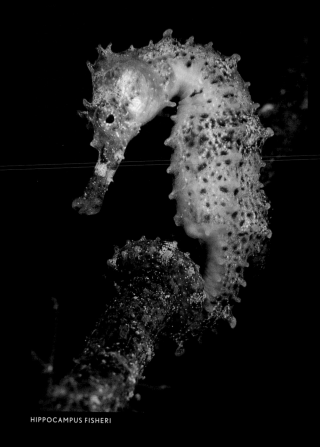

HIPPOCAMPUS FISHERI

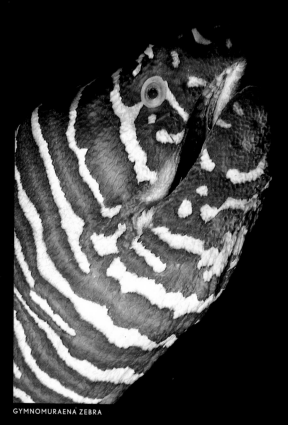

GYMNOMURAENA ZEBRA

GYMNOTHORAX MELATREMUS

ANICULUS MAXIMUS; SHELL OF TONNA PERDIX

Although not technically reef dwellers, giant trevally or ulua aukea spend enough time on the reef hunting fishes and hovering over cleaning stations that divers and snorkelers have many opportunities to see them. These powerful jacks are extremely fast and when a small reef fish has managed to make it to cover, the jack might circle over the fish's hole for several minutes, seemingly agitated over its defeat.

CARANX IGNOBILIS

CHAETODON MILIARIS

A school of milletseed butterflyfish (lau-wiliwili) and a school of raccoon butterflyfish (kīkākapu) have attacked a Hawaiian sergeant nest, left, and the male was unable to chase them off. Butterflyfish school not just for safety, but also to be better able to overwhelm the defenses of other fishes. In this photograph at least the milletseeds seem to have achieved the better feeding position. Their mouths are perfectly shaped for plucking up the little morsels (top). Two male Hawaiian sergeants guard a patch of purple eggs (right). Several nests are laid at the same time and in close proximity to each other (below). This way if a school of fish approaches, there are many Hawaiian sergeants to drive it off, instead of just one. Also, if the school is able to overwhelm one of the sergeants and attack his nest, the fish can eat only so many eggs, and other nests will escape predation. Not recorded in Hawai'i until 1992, the Indo-Pacific sergeant (bottom right) appears to be a recent colonizer that is here to stay. Closely related to the Hawaiian sergeant, it may be the ancestor species from which the Hawaiian sergeant evolved. The new arrivals feed and nest among the Hawaiian sergeants, but appear to spawn only with each other.

ABUDEFDUF ABDOMINALIS

ABUDEFDUF ABDOMINALIS

ABUDEFDUF VAIGIENSIS

ELAGATIS BIPINNULATUS

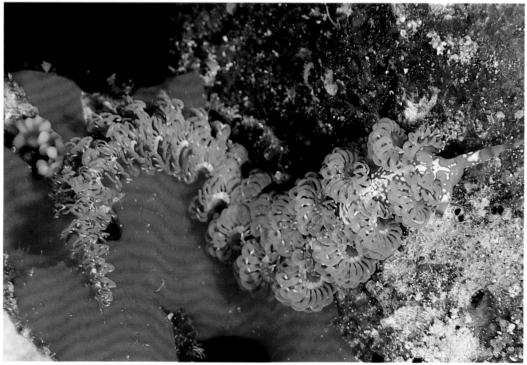

PTERAEOLIDIA IANTHINA

SYNODUS VARIEGATUS

Camouflaged species, such as these variegated lizardfish or 'ulae (above), frequently stay very close, even touching, during the hours prior to spawning. When the female gets up to move due to a disturbance, the male follows immediately, settling right next to or even on top of the female. The impressive array of teeth is useful for capturing fishes, shrimps, and squids, which the lizardfish darts up from the bottom to snatch. Rainbow runners or kamanu (top left) are actually streamlined and powerful jacks that hunt for small fishes and planktonic crustaceans in open water. Because of their exposed lifestyle, they often form large schools for protection, but may also be seen traveling alone. Protected by stinging cells on the curly projections of its back, the blue dragon nudibranch (left) can remain exposed without much threat. Fish that take a bite, quickly learn of its defense and the nudibranch regenerates its missing end. These stinging cells are obtained when the nudibranch eats hydroids. Produced by the hydroids, the stinging cells pass through the digestive system of the nudibranch and are stored for later use. Also contained within the projections are symbiotic algae. By arranging the projections to maximize exposure to the sun, the nudibranch is provided with a supply of food produced by the algae.

TAMBJA MOROSA

The beautiful long-tailed sea hare (left) was named for its extremely long foot, the end of which is adhesive for clinging to debris floating on the ocean's surface (which can be a rough environment). It survives by grazing on algae which is plentiful on drifting objects exposed to so much sunlight. This velvet nudibranch (above right) is laying its brilliant orange eggs on a winged oyster. Nudibranchs have both male and female sex organs, and when copulating, sperm is exchanged. Afterward, each nudibranch can lay at least one fertilized egg mass, and usually more. Bicolor anthias (center right) live in a harem, as do other basslets, with one male dominating several females. This is a male, as can be seen from the elongated second and third dorsal spines. The spines have yellow tufts at the ends, and look somewhat like antennae. During the day, these anthias hover above the bottom picking plankton from the water. Hundreds of fleshy projections augment the already fabulous camouflage of the titan scorpionfish or nohu, by breaking up its outline (bottom right). At depth, the colors are lost and the fish matches the algae-covered rock. This is Hawai'i's largest scorpionfish, reaching almost two feet in length.

PSEUDANTHIAS BICOLOR

SCORPAENOPSIS CACOPSIS

HETEROCENTROTUS MAMMILLATUS

MEGAPTERA NOVAEANGLIAE

AETOBATIS NARINARI

During whale season, humpback whales or koholā (above) approach Molokini often, and even enter the crater periodically. The calves, born here in Hawai'i, are so curious that they sometimes approach divers and snorkelers, and naturally the mothers follow closely behind. Although such an experience is extremely rare and completely unpredictable, many divers and snorkelers have been in the right place at the right time to witness what may be the most magnificent creature in Hawaiian waters. Remember that humpbacks are endangered, and by law may not be approached within one hundred yards by any means. Encounters are totally dependent upon the whales approaching us. Rooting in the bottom with its pig-like snout, the spotted eagle ray or hīhīmanu (below left) is searching for mollusks and crustaceans, which it crushes with jaws powerful enough to crack even very hard shells. The ray is still able to breathe while its snout is buried because water is drawn in through a large hole just above and behind each eye and expelled through the gill slits on the underside of the body. This is one of three shallow water rays found in Hawai'i that are capable of defending themselves with venomous barbs on the tail. The red pencil urchin or hā'uke'uke'ula'ula (left) lives in the shallow surge zone along the outer rim. Here the high light levels and heavy water movement discourage coral growth, and encourage algae, which it eats.

PHYLLIDIA SP.

The banded spiny lobster or ula (left) keeps its tail under a coral shelf, facing the world with its tough antennae. A female of the same species (right), carries as many as 500,000 eggs. In this photograph, she is aerating them by flapping her swimmerets and by moving her hindmost pair of legs among them. She will tend them in this manner for a month, until they hatch and join the plankton as larvae. Also clearly visible in this photo are clusters of commensal goose neck barnacles which are living on the mouthparts of the lobster. When the lobster eats, these filter feeders sift the crumbs of their host's meal. Resembling the common varicose nudibranch, the undescribed Phyllidia above similarly advertises its toxic content with a striking color pattern. If fishes ignore the warning and eat the nudibranch anyway, they will spit it out, having learned a valuable lesson about animals with bright contrasting colors. Because of its tough body, the Phyllidia is often unharmed during the fish's learning process.

LOBSTER: PANULIRUS MARGINATUS; BARNACLES: PARALEPAS SP.

LIOPROPOMA AURORA

The little wire coral shrimp (opposite) lives among the coral's polyps, well camouflaged by the bars on its body. It picks at mucus and plankton that have drifted into the coral's tentacles. Usually found in pairs, the female is the larger of the two and is often seen carrying eggs. The sunset basslet (above) is one of several deepwater fishes that sometimes inhabits shallow water at Molokini. As a member of the grouper family, it has the characteristic pear-shaped pupils. Solitary individuals living at Molokini spend their days under ledges over one hundred feet down, emerging to feed. This rare fish is found only in Hawai'i.

Manta rays live most of their lives in the open ocean. When this ray approached Molokini, jacks (which normally feed on smaller reef fish) attacked the remoras hitchhiking behind the manta's cephalic fins. With nowhere to hide, the remoras were shredded by the attacking jacks, and finally torn from the ray.

MANTA BIROSTRIS
JACKS: CARANX IGNOBILIS
REMORAS: REMORINA ALBESCENS

PTEROIS SPHEX

Long legs terminating in a hook are characteristic of the colorful long-handed spiny lobster (left). Typically living in water below 100 feet, the front halves of their bodies extend from holes during the day. At night they roam over the bottom. With its exotic pectoral fins spread, the Hawaiian turkeyfish or nohu pinao (above) looks threatening, especially to one who has experienced its venom. The venom, which is injected through the dorsal spines, causes extreme pain in the injured area for several hours, but is rarely deadly to humans. The pair of fleshy tentacles on the head are present in some individuals and not in others. They are not related to the sex or maturity of the fish. Turkeyfish are nocturnal and feed on small shrimps and crabs. Hovering just off the underside off a ledge, groups of tiny Taylor's gobies (middle right) pick copepods from the water. They will quickly retreat to the shelter of crevices when threatened. In the foreground is a male, identified by the longer dorsal spine. To see these fish requires keen eyes. This male redstripe pipefish (right) is carrying eggs on its abdomen, a strange but normal procedure for pipefishes and seahorses, which are in the same family. As the eggs mature over a period of weeks, they will change color from pink to dark silver. When they hatch as larvae from the egg cases, they are on their own. The male is then ready to accept a new batch of eggs from the female, which he then fertilizes.

TRIMMA TAYLORI

DUNCKEROCAMPUS BALDWINI

GOBY: PLEUROSICYA MICHELI; CORAL: LEPTOSERIS HAWAIIENSIS

GENICANTHUS PERSONATUS (FEMALE)

THYSANOSTOMA SP.

,Michel's goby (above left) actually specializes in living on hard corals. Able to withstand the coral's stinging cells, the goby occupies a niche that other fishes may find unacceptable. This species of coral is typically deep-dwelling, and grows on the vertical surfaces of the outer wall. This drifting pelagic jellyfish (above) is protected by stinging cells, and not as vulnerable as it looks. Protection is not absolute however, as some of the oral arms are occasionally nipped off by fishes. As it drifts, or swims along, it is also eating. Plankton that is trapped in mucus is digested by many mouths located along the arms. The endemic masked angelfish (left), common in the northwestern Hawaiian Islands, is almost never seen by divers in the main islands. However, Molokini's unique situation and habitats have allowed a few to take up residence over the years. A couple even come in shallow enough for divers to see. This female appeared in 1997 and spent her days picking plankton and grazing algae from the rocks. Beginning life as females, angelfishes can change to male if the social situation warrants. Because she was never joined by any of her kind, this one lived out her life as a female. In a frozen moment (right), two species—an aeolid nudibranch and a squat lobster—occupy the same tiny space on the bottom. Neither has yet been described. Small species such as these escape official recognition because of their diminutive size and sparse distribution on the reef.

NUDIBRANCH: PHIDIANA SP;. SQUAT LOBSTER: GALATHEA SP.

EVISTIAS ACUTIROSTRIS

Traveling as a school, these orangespine unicornfish or umaumalei (right) stop en masse to graze on algae, then all move on to the next stop. The two fixed spines on either side of the orangespine unicornfish's tail are accented with brilliant orange to advertise their potential harm. Males can be identified by the long filaments trailing from their tail fins, and appear to take position at the top of the school. Perhaps because it is suited to the cooler water, the unusual boarfish (left) is rarely found at Molokini, and only in the deep. Off Kaua'i and up in the northwestern Hawaiian Islands it lives in much shallower water. It retreats under ledges during the day and emerges at night to feed on brittlestars and other invertebrates. The unusual black color of the reticulated butterflyfish (below left) makes it easy to identify, but unfortunately it is rarely seen. Only two pairs are currently known to reside at Molokini. They both live along the outer wall, feeding on coral polyps and algae during the day.

CHAETODON RETICULATUS

NASO HEXACANTHUS

PSEUDANTHIAS HAWAIIENSIS

This male Hawaiian longfin anthias (right) displays the extremely long pelvic fins for which the species was named. Like fairies, the longfin anthias (above) hover just over the rocky bottom, plucking their food from the water column. At center left, with a light lavender tail, the lone male is looking at the photographer with suspicion. He manages a large harem of females, in this case at least 24! He prevents other males from approaching and spawning with them. When the male dies, the female of highest rank will change sex (in as little as two weeks) and become the new male for the harem. Finding protection in numbers, sleek unicornfish or ʻōpelu kala (top) pick plankton from the water column next to the outer wall. At certain times of the year they form massive aggregations, the larger males flashing blue stripes on their faces and appearing to chase females, in apparent courtship activity.

MONACHIS SCHAUINSLANDI

STENOPUS PYRSONOTUS

CORAL: CARIJOA RIISEI; BUTTERFLYFISH: CHAETODON MILIARIS

Fountain shrimp (above) are not frequently seen by divers, and are usually found living in pairs. This pair lived in a small alcove along the outer rim for three years. During that time the female (in back) brooded a new batch of eggs for three weeks every month during the entire three years. The eggs, as here, show turquoise. The critically endangered Hawaiian monk seal (top left) is one of only two species of monk seals remaining worldwide. This particular seal, a young male, visited Molokini many times from 1997 to 1999, and sought out divers and snorkelers for interaction. At other times it could be seen resting on the exposed wave bench inside the crescent. Monk seals feed on fishes, octopuses, and spiny lobsters, and years ago one was photographed at Molokini slurping down a large moray eel. Snowflake coral (left) is one of Hawai'i's few conspicuous soft corals. Not native to the islands, it was probably introduced during the mid-70's. Most of the soft white polyps are closed during the day, as in this photo, but open at night when plankton are more numerous, and during the day when current is present. Milletseed butterflyfish use the coral for shelter while also picking plankton.

Using fins specialized for perching, this longnose hawkfish rests among the branches of black corals, where its crosshatch pattern blends well. It scans the water for plankton which it plucks with its distinctive snout.
OXYCIRRHITES TYPUS

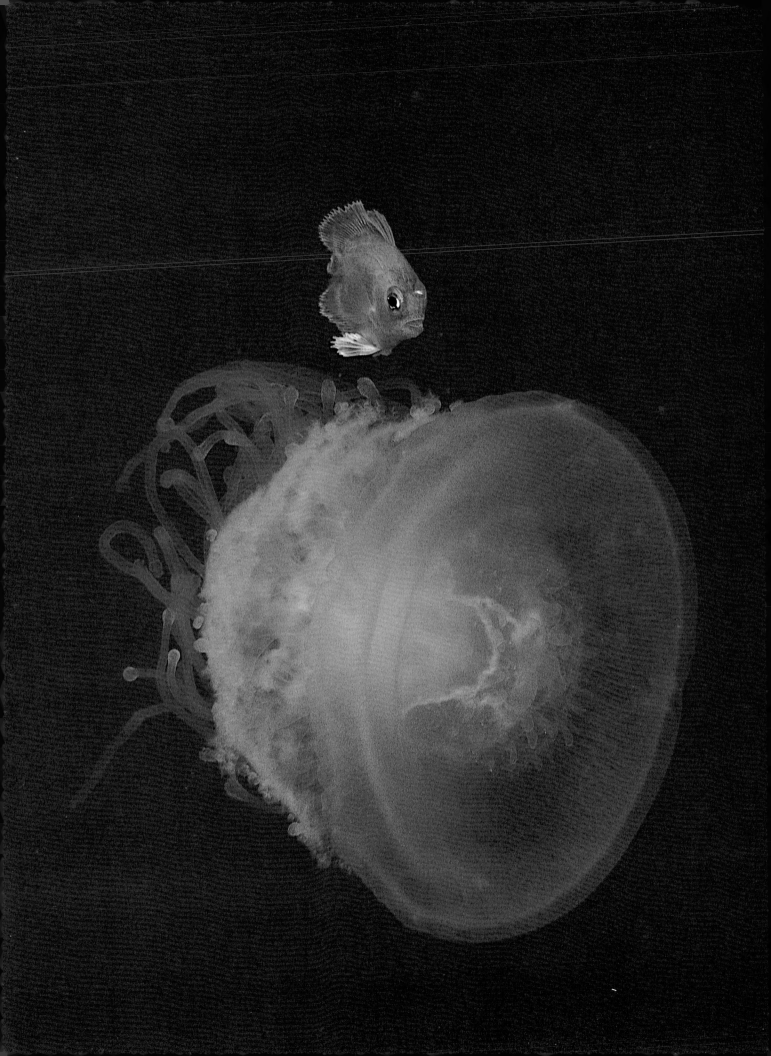

Conservation Note

The Molokini Marine Life Conservation District (MLCD) is one link in a chain of protected areas in Hawai'i, necessary for the conservation and replenishment of marine resources. Habitat degradation is caused by activities onshore and fishing pressure from an increasing population with greater technology. It is estimated that at least thirty percent of coral reefs worldwide should be set aside and protected from all forms of harvesting in order to preserve the integrity of coral reef ecosystems. These areas allow the animals to reach sexual maturity and seed other areas where fishing and harvesting are allowed.

While the vast majority of people respect Molokini's protected status, there are still a few who close their eyes to the big picture of overall health of Hawai'i's ecosystems for immediate personal gratification. Occasional fishers still breach the sanctuary boundaries when other boaters are not around to monitor the crater. With increased public awareness, respect for these few protected areas will grow and Molokini, as well as other protected areas, will be the sanctuaries they were intended to be.

Molokini is one of ten MLCDs in Hawai'i. Designated by the state's Department of Natural Resources, MLCDs are intended to conserve and replenish Hawai'i's marine resources, while at the same time provide access to people who wish to observe Hawai'i's beautiful marine life. Because the animals in MLCDs are protected and because they are accustomed to the presence of divers and snorkelers, MLCDs are often the best areas to get close to fish and photograph them.

Below are the current MLCDs on each island. While rules for each differ (some prohibit boats and fishing of any kind while others, like Molokini, allow boats and limited fishing), it is generally prohibited to take any living material or non-living habitat material (rocks, sand, coral skeletons). Therefore it is probably best to avoid any consumptive activities within the protected areas. Complete rules are available from the Division of Aquatic Resources, 1151 Punchbowl Street, Honolulu, HI 96813.

Many small fishes take shelter among the tentacles and oral arms of jellyfishes during their juvenile stages. The medusa fish, however, lives with jellyfishes throughout its life, specializing in this very narrow habitat. When small, it is able to dive up inside the jellyfish's oral arms, but as an adult of four inches, it can only draw up against the bottom of the jellyfish for protection.

Hawai'i's Marine Life Conservation Districts

Maui
Molokini Shoal
Honolua-Mokule'ia

O'ahu
Hanauma Bay
Pupukea
Waikiki

Hawai'i
Kealakekua Bay
Lapakahi
Old Kona Airport
Waialea Bay

Lana'i
Manele-Hulopo'e

Fish Species Recorded from Molokini

Family Rhincodontidae
Whale Sharks
  Rhincodon typus

Family Carcharhinidae
Requiem Sharks
  Carcharhinus amblyrhynchos
  Carcharhinus melanopterus
  Galeocerdo cuvier

Family Hemigaleidae
Weasel Sharks
  Triaenodon obesus

Family Sphyrnidae
Hammerhead Sharks
  Sphyrna leweni

Family Myliobatidae
Eagle Rays
  Aetobatis narinari

Family Mobulidae
Manta Rays
  Manta birostris

Family Muraenidae
Morays
  Echidna nebulosa
  Enchelycore pardalis
  Enchelynassa canina
  Gymnomuraena zebra
  Gymnothorax eurostus
  Gymnothorax flavimarginatus
  Gymnothorax gracilicaudus
  Gymnothorax melatremus
  Gymnothorax meleagris
  Gymnothorax undulatus
  Scuticaria bennettii
  Scuticaria tigrina

Family Ophichthidae
Snake Eels
  Apterichtus flavicaudus
  Brachysomophis crocodilinus
  Callechelys lutea
  Myrichthys magnificus

Family Congridae
Conger Eels
  Conger cinereus
  Gorgasia hawaiiensis
  Poeciloconger fasciatus

Family Engraulidae
Anchovies
  Encrasicholina sp.

Family Synodontidae
Lizardfishes
  Saurida flamma
  Synodus binotatus
  Synodus dermatogenys
  Synodus ulae
  Synodus variegatus

Family Ophidiidae
Brotulas
  Brotula multibarbata

Family Antennariidae
Frogfishes
  Antennarius pictus
  Antennarius commerson
  Antennatus tuberosus
  Histrio histrio

Family Belonidae
Needlefishes
  Strongylura appendiculata
  Tylosurus crocodilus

Family Hemiramphidae (Halfbeaks)
  Hyporhamphus acutus

Family Holocentridae
Squirrelfishes and Soldierfishes
  Myripristis amaena
  Myripristis berndti
  Myripristis chryseres
  Myripristis kuntee
  Myripristis vittata
  Neoniphon aurolineatus
  Plectrypops lima
  Sargocentron ensiferum
  Sargocentron iota
  Sargocentron spiniferum
  Sargocentron tiere
  Sargocentron xantherythrum

Family Aulostomidae
Trumpetfishes
  Aulostomus chinensis

Family Fistulariidae
Cornetfishes
  Fistularia commersonii

Family Syngnathidae
Pipefishes and Seahorses
  Doryrhamphus excisus
  Dunckerocampus baldwini
  Hippocampus fisheri

Family Scorpaenidae
Scorpionfishes
  Dendrochirus barberi
  Iracundus signifer
  Pterois sphex
  Scorpaenopsis cacopsis
  Scorpaenopsis diabolus
  Sebastapistes coniorta
  Taenianotus triacanthus

Family Dactylopteridae
Flying Gurnards
  Dactyloptena orientalis

Family Caracanthidae
Velvetfishes
  Caracanthus typicus

Family Serranidae
Groupers, Basslets, and Anthias
  Cephalopholis argus
  Epinephelus lanceolatus
  Holanthias elizabethae
  Holanthias fuscipinnis
  Liopropoma aurora
  Pseudanthias bicolor
  Pseudanthias hawaiiensis
  Pseudanthias thompsoni

Family Kuhliidae
Flagtails
  Kuhlia xenura

Family Priacanthidae
Bigeyes
  Heteropriacanthus cruentatus
  Priacanthus meeki

Family Cirrhitidae (Hawkfishes)
  Amblycirrhitus bimacula
  Cirrhitops fasciatus
  Cirrhitus pinnulatus
  Oxycirrhites typus
  Paracirrhites arcatus
  Paracirrhites forsteri

Family Apogonidae
Cardinalfishes
  Apogon kallopterus
  Apogon menesemus

Family Malacanthidae
Tilefishes
  Malacanthus brevirostris

Family Echeneidae
Remoras
  Remorina albescens

Family Carangidae
Jacks
  Alectis ciliaris
  Carangoides ferdau
  Carangoides orthogrammus
  Caranx ignobilis
  Caranx lugubris
  Caranx melampygus
  Caranx sexfasciatus
  Decapterus macarellus
  Elagatis bipinnulata
  Scomberoides lysan
  Selar crumenophthalmus
  Seriola dumerili

Family Nomeidae
Driftfishes
  Psenes arafuraensis

Family Lutjanidae
Snappers
  Aphareus furca
  Aprion virescens
  Lutjanus fulvus
  Lutjanus kasmira

Family Lethrinidae
Emperors
  Monotaxis grandoculis

Family Mullidae
Goatfishes
  Mulloidichthys flavolineatus
  Mulloidichthys pflugeri
  Mulloidichthys vanicolensis
  Parupeneus bifasciatus
  Parupeneus cyclostomus
  Parupeneus multifasciatus
  Parupeneus pleurostigma
  Parupeneus porphyreus

Family Kyphosidae
Sea Chubs
  Kyphosus bigibbus
  Kyphosus cinerascens
  Kyphosus vaigiensis

Family Chaetodontidae
Butterflyfishes
  Chaetodon auriga
  Chaetodon fremblii
  Chaetodon kleinii
  Chaetodon lunula
  Chaetodon lunulatus
  Chaetodon miliaris
  Chaetodon multicinctus
  Chaetodon ornatissimus
  Chaetodon quadrimaculatus
  Chaetodon reticulatus
  Chaetodon tinkeri

Chaetodon trifascialis
Chaetodon unimaculatus
Forcipiger flavissimus
Forcipiger longirostris
Hemitaurichthys polylepis
Hemitaurichthys thompsoni
Heniochus diphreutes

Family Pomacanthidae
Angelfishes
  Centropyge fisheri
  Centropyge loricula
  Centropyge potteri
  Desmoholacanthus arcuatus
  Genicanthus personatus

Family Pentacerotidae
Boarfishes
  Evistias acutirostris

Family Pomacentridae
Damselfishes
  Abudefduf abdominalis
  Abudefduf sordidus
  Abudefduf vaigiensis
  Chromis agilis
  Chromis hanui
  Chromis leucura
  Chromis ovalis
  Chromis vanderbilti
  Chromis verater
  Dascyllus albisella
  Plectroglyphidodon imparipennis
  Plectroglyphidodon johnstonianus
  Stegastes fasciolatus

Family Labridae
Wrasses
  Anampses chrysocephalus
  Anampses cuvier
  Bodianus bilunulatus
  Cheilio inermis
  Cirrhilabrus jordani
  Coris ballieui
  Coris flavovittata
  Coris gaimard
  Coris venusta
  Cymolutes lecluse
  Gomphosus varius
  Halichoeres ornatissimus
  Labroides phthirophagus
  Macropharyngodon geoffroy
  Novaculichthys taeniourus
  Novaculichthys woodi
  Oxycheilinus bimaculatus
  Oxycheilinus unifasciatus
  Pseudocheilinus evanidus
  Pseudocheilinus octotaenia
  Pseudocheilinus tetrataenia

Pseudojuloides cerasinus
Stethojulis balteata
Thalassoma ballieui
Thalassoma duperrey
Thalassoma lutescens
Thalassoma purpureum
Thalassoma quinquevittatum
Thalassoma trilobatum
Xyrichtys aneitensis
Xyrichtys pavo

Family Scaridae
Parrotfishes
  Calotomus carolinus
  Chlorurus perspicillatus
  Chlorurus sordidus
  Scarus dubius
  Scarus psittacus
  Scarus rubroviolaceus

Family Callionymidae
Dragonets
  Callionymus sp.

Family Pinguipedidae
Sandperches
  Parapercis schauinslandii

Family Blenniidae
Blennies
  Cirripectes obscurus
  Cirripectes vanderbilti
  Entomacrodus marmoratus
  Exallias brevis
  Plagiotremus ewaensis
  Plagiotremus goslinei

Family Gobiidae
Gobies
  Bryaninops yongei
  Pleurosicya micheli
  Pleurosicya sp.
  Priolepis aureoviridis
  Priolepis sp.
  Trimma taylori

Family Microdesmidae
Dartfishes and Wormfishes
  Nemateleotris magnifica
  Ptereleotris heteroptera

Family Zanclidae
Moorish Idols
  Zanclus cornutus

Family Acanthuridae
Surgeonfishes
  Acanthurus achilles
  Acanthurus blochii
  Acanthurus dussumieri
  Acanthurus guttatus

Acanthurus leucopareius
Acanthurus nigricans
Acanthurus nigrofuscus
Acanthurus nigroris
Acanthurus olivaceus
Acanthurus triostegus
Acanthurus xanthopterus
Ctenochaetus hawaiiensis
Ctenochaetus strigosus
Naso annulatus
Naso brevirostris
Naso caesius
Naso hexacanthus
Naso lituratus
Naso maculatus
Naso unicornis
Zebrasoma flavescens
Zebrasoma veliferum

Family Sphyraenidae
Barracudas
Sphyraena barracuda
Sphyraena helleri

Family Bothidae
Lefteye Flounders
Bothus mancus
Bothus pantherinus

Family Scombridae
Tunas and Mackerels
Acanthocybium solandri
Euthynnus affinus
Neothunnus albacares

Family Balistidae
Triggerfishes
Canthidermis maculatus
Melichthys niger
Melichthys vidua
Rhinecanthus rectangulus
Sufflamen bursa
Sufflamen fraenatus
Xanthichthys auromarginatus
Xanthichthys caeruleolineatus
Xanthichthys mento

Family Monacanthidae
Filefishes
Aluterus scriptus
Cantherhines dumerilii
Cantherhines sandwichiensis
Cantherhines verecundus
Pervagor aspricaudus
Pervagor spilosoma

Family Ostraciidae
Trunkfishes
Lactophrys diaphanus
Lactoria fornasini

Ostracion meleagris
Ostracion whitleyi

Family Tetraodontidae
Puffers
Arothron hispidus
Arothron meleagris
Canthigaster amboinensis
Canthigaster coronata

Canthigaster epilampra
Canthigaster jactator

Family Diodontidae
Porcupinefishes
Chilomycterus reticulatus
Diodon holocanthus
Diodon hystrix

Coral Species Recorded from Molokini

ORDER SCLERACTINIA
Stony Corals

Family Acroporidae
Montipora capitata
Montipora flabellata
Montipora incrassata
Montipora patula

Family Astrocoeniidae
Madracis pharensis

Family Pocilloporidae
Pocillopora damicornis
Pocillopora meandrina
Pocillopora ligulata
Pocillopora eydouxi

Family Siderastreidae
Coscinaraea wellsi
Psammocora stellata
Psammocora explanulata

Family Agariciidae
Pavona varians
Pavona duerdeni
Pavona maldivensis
Leptoseris incrustans
Leptoseris hawaiiensis
Leptoseris mycetoseroides
Leptoseris tubulifera

Family Fungiidae
Diaseris fragilis
Fungia granulosa
Fungia scutaria
Cycloseris vaughani

Family Dendrophylliidae
Cladopsammia eguchii
Tubastrea coccinea
Tubastrea diaphana
Rhizopsammia verrilli

Family Caryophylliidae
Tethocyathus minor

Family Faviidae
Cyphastrea agassizi
Cyphastrea ocellina
Leptastrea bewickensis
Leptastrea purpurea

Family Poritidae
Porites compressa
Porites lobata
Porites brighami
Porites evermanni
Porites rus
Porites cf. studeri
Porites sp.

ORDER ANTIPATHARIA
Black Corals
Antipathes intermedia
Antipathes dichotoma
Antipathes grandis
Antipathes ulex
Cirrhipathes anguina
Stichopathes cf. echinata

Identifications by Jim Maragos, Doug Fenner, Steven Cairns, J.E.N. Veron, and Cory Pittman. The list follows the usage in Fenner (2002).

Bibliography

Allen, Gerald R., 1975. *Damselfishes of the South Seas*. 1975. Neptune City, N.J: THF Publications, Inc.

———, Roger Steene and M. Allen. 1998. *A Guide to Angelfishes and Butterflyfishes*. Odyssey Publishing/Tropical Reef Research.

——— and A.R. Emery, 1985. *A Review of the Pomacentrid Fishes of the Genus Stegastes from the Indo-Pacific*. Indo-Pacific Fishes, No. 3. Honolulu: B.P. Bishop Museum Press.

Anon., 1917. "Gooding Field Boosting Maui's Coral Gardens." *Maui News*, April 27, A8.

———, 1926. "Gymnastics Found Necessary When Exploring Little Islet of Molokini." *Maui News*, July 31, A1.

———, 1975. Aerial photograph. *Honolulu Advertiser*, Jun 10, F8.

———, 1977. "Molokini 'Restricted' Starting Tomorrow." *Honolulu Advertiser*, July 7, A3.

———, 1984. "Divers Move Two Bombs." *Honolulu Advertiser*, June 12, C2.

———, 1984. "Maui's Molokini—One Small Island." *Honolulu Star Bulletin*, Dec. 9, A18.

Apple, Russ., 1983. "The Barren Islet of Molokini." *Honolulu Star Bulletin*, May 27, A22.

——— and Peg Apple, 1974. "Lonely Molokini." *Honolulu Star Bulletin*, June 29, A11.

Arago, Jacques, 1823. *Narrative of a Voyage Round the World*. London: Treuttel and Wurtz.

Ashdown, Inez, 1960. "Molokini and the Mo'o Maiden." *Honolulu Star Bulletin*, June 26, A23.

———, 1989. "The Legend of Black Coral." *Pacific Art and Travel*, Autumn.

Benson, Bruce, 1975. "2 Bombs Explode Into Spat." *Honolulu Advertiser*, July 29, A6.

Berger, Andrew J., 1972. *Hawaiian Birdlife*. Honolulu: The University of Hawai'i Press.

Bertsch, Hans and Scott Johnson, 1981. *Hawaiian Nudibranchs*. Honolulu: Oriental Publishing.

Buck, Paul H., 1936. "Report of the Director." B.P. Bishop Museum Bulletin 149(17).Honolulu: B.P. Bishop Museum Press.

———, 1964. "Arts and Crafts of Hawai'i." *B.P. Bishop Museum Special Publication 45(VII) Fishing*. Honolulu: B.P. Bishop Museum Press.

Carlson, Bruce A., 1992. *Life History and Reproductive Success of Exallias brevis*. Ph.D. thesis, University of Hawai'i.

Carpenter, Russell and Blyth Carpenter., 1981. *Fish Watching in Hawai'i*. San Mateo, California: Natural World Press.

Carson, Hampton L. and David A. Clague, 1995. *Geology and Biogeography of the Hawaiian Islands*. Hawaiian Biogeography. Eds. Warren L. Wagner and V.A. Funk. Washington: Smithsonian Institution Press.

Castillo, Stephanie, 1984. "Small Isle Site of Big Dispute." *Honolulu Star Bulletin*, Dec. 17, A1.

Caum, Edward L., 1930. "Notes on the Flora of Molokini." *B.P. Bishop Museum Occasional Papers 9(1)*. Honolulu: B.P. Bishop Museum Press.

Childs, Jeff, 1998. "Nocturnal Mooring and Parking Behavior of Three Monacanthids (Filefishes) at an Offshore Production Platform in the Northwestern Gulf of Mexico." *Gulf of Mexico Science* 16(2).

Clarke, Gar, 1982. *A Botanical Reconnaissance of Molokini Island*. Hawai'i Department of Land and Natural resources, Division of Forestry.

Crowley, Thomas J. and Gerald R. North, 1991. *Paleoclimatology*. New York: Oxford University Press.

Devaney, Dennis M., and Lucius G. Eldredge, eds., 1977. *Reef and Shore Fauna of Hawai'i. Section 1: Protozoa through Ctenophora*. Honolulu: B.P. Bishop Museum Press.

———, 1987. *Reef and Shore Fauna of Hawai'i. Section 2: Platyhelminthes through Phoronida and Section 3: Sipuncula through Annelida*. Honolulu: B.P. Bishop Museum Press.

Edmonson, Charles H., 1922. "Hawaiian Dromiidae." *B.P. Bishop Museum Occasional Papers*, 8(2). Honolulu: B.P. Bishop Museum Press.

———, 1954. "Hawaiian Portunidae." *B.P. Bishop Museum Occasional Papers*, 21(12). Honolulu: B.P. Bishop Museum Press.

———, 1933. "Reef and Shore Fauna of Hawai'i." *B.P. Bishop Museum Occasional Papers*, 22.

———, 1962. "Xanthidae of Hawai'i." B.P. Bishop Museum Occasional Papers, 22(13).

Fenner, D. 2002. *Corals of Hawai'i, Field Guide to the Hard, Soft, and Black Corals of Hawai'i and the Northwest Hawaiian Islands, including Midway*. Sea Challengers, Monterey.

Fiene, Pauline, 1998. "A Note on Synchronous Spawning in the Reef Coral *Pocillopora meandrina* at Molokini Islet, Hawai'i." University of Hawai'i. Hawai'i Institute of Marine Biology Technical Report No. 42.

Fletcher, Charles H. et. al. 1994. *Sea-level Change in Hawai'i*. SOEST Report 1993–94. School of Ocean and Earth Science and Technology, University of Hawai'i.

Forbes, C.N., 1913. "Notes on the Flora of Kaho'olawe and Molokini." *B.P. Bishop Museum Occasional Papers*, 5(3). Honolulu: B.P. Bishop Museum Press.

Fornander, Abraham, 1916–1917. "Collection of Hawaiian Antiquities and Folk-lore." Ed. T.G. Thrum. *Bernice Pauahi Bishop Museum Memoir*, 4(1). Honolulu: B.P. Bishop Museum Press.

————, 1919. "Collection of Hawaiian Antiquities and Folk-lore." Ed. T.G. Thrum. *B.P. Bishop Museum Memoir*, 5(3). Honolulu: B.P. Bishop Museum Press.

Gosliner, Terrence M. and Rebecca F. Johnson, 1999. "Phylogeny of *Hypselodoris* (Nudibranchia: Chromodorididae) with a review of the monophyletic clade of Indo-Pacific species, Including descriptions of twelve new species." *Zoological Journal of the Linnean Society,* 125: 1–114.

Hanlon, Roger T. and John B. Messenger, 1996. *Cephalopod Behavior.* Cambridge: Cambridge University Press.

Harrison, Craig S., 1990. *Seabirds of Hawai'i.* Ithaca, New York: Cornell University Press.

Hobdy, Robert W., 1982. "Vegetation of Molokini Islet." Unpublished.

————, 1987. "*Portulaca molokiniensis* (Portulacaceae), a New Species from the Hawaiian Islands." *Pacific Science,* 41(1–4).

Hoover, John P., 1998. *Hawai'i's Sea Creatures. A Guide to Hawai'i's Marine Invertebrates.* Honolulu: Mutual Publishing.

Hunter, Cynthia L. and Jennifer E. Smith, 1998. "Marine Algae Collection Report—Molokini Shoal MLCD." Unpublished.

Kamakau, Samuel M., 1976. *The Works of the People of Old.* B.P. Bishop Museum Special Publication 61. Honolulu: B.P. Bishop Museum Press.

Kapakapa, Inoa, 1940. "Island of Molokini." *Paradise of the Pacific,* 52(2):12

Kay, E. Alison, 1972. *A Natural History of the Hawaiian Islands.* Honolulu: University Press of Hawai'i.

————, 1979. "Hawaiian Marine Shells." *Reef and Shore Fauna of Hawai'i, Sec. 4: Mollusca.* Honolulu: B.P. Bishop Museum Press.

Kepler, Cameron B. and Angela K. Kepler, 1980. "The Birds of Molokini Island, Maui." *'Elepaio,* 40(11).

LaPerouse, Jean F., 1968. *Voyage Round the World,* Vol. 1. Amsterdam: Da Capo Press.

Lourie, Sara A., Amanda C.J. Vincent and H.J. Hall, 1999. *Seahorses: An Identification Guide to the World's Species and Their Conservation.* London: Project Seahorse.

Macdonald, Gordon A., 1972. *Volcanoes.* Englewood Cliffs: Prentice- Hall, Inc.

———— and Agatin T. Abbott, 1970. *Volcanoes in the Sea: The Geology of Hawai'i.* Honolulu: University Press of Hawai'i.

Maragos, James E., 1977. *Reef and Shore Fauna of Hawai'i. Sec. 1: Protozoa through Ctenophora. Order Scleractinia: Stony Corals.* Eds. D.M. Devaney and L.G. Eldredge. Honolulu: B.P. Bishop Museum Press. pp. 158–241.

Michael, Scott W. 1998. *Reef Fishes: A Guide to Their Identification, Behavior, and Captive Care.* Vol. 1. Shelburne, Vermont: Microcosm Ltd.

Miller, Ken, 1988. "Divers Finally Complete Installation of Mooring Pins at Molokini." *Honolulu Star Bulletin*, April 26, A4.

————, 1988. "Navy Trying to Remove Molokini Bombs." *Honolulu Star Bulletin*, Aug. 10, A6.

Myers, Robert F., 1999. *Micronesian Reef Fishes.* 3rd Edition. Barrigada, Guam: Coral Graphics.

Palmer, Harold S., 1930. "Geology of Molokini." *B.P. Bishop Museum Occasional Papers.* 9(1). Honolulu: B.P. Bishop Museum Press.

Pietsch, Theodore W. and David B. Grobecker, 1987. *Frogfishes of the World.* Stanford: Stanford University Press.

Pukui, Mary K. and Samuel H. Elbert, 1965. *Hawaiian Dictionary.* Honolulu: The University Press of Hawai'i.

————, Samuel H. Elbert and E.T. Mookini, 1974. *Place Names of Hawai'i.* Honolulu: The University Press of Hawai'i.

Randall, John E., 1985. *Guide to Hawaiian Reef Fishes.* Newton Square, Pennsylvania: Harrowood Books.

————, 1996. *Shore Fishes of Hawai'i.* Vida, Oregon: Natural World Press.

———— and L Taylor. 1988. *A Review of the Indo-Pacific Fishes of the Serranid Genus Liopropoma, with Descriptions of Seven New Species.* Indo-Pacific Fishes, no. 16. B.P. Honolulu: Bishop Museum Press.

————, Gerald R. Allen and R.C. Steene. 1990. *Fishes of the Great Barrier Reef and Coral Sea.* Honolulu: University of Hawai'i Press.

Ruppert, Edward E. and Robert D. Barnes, 1994. *Invertebrate Zoology.* 6th ed. Saunders College Publ.

Ryan, Tim, 1984. "Plan for Detonation off Molokini Island." *Honolulu Star Bulletin*, Nov. 15, A23.

Sahm, Leo, 1911. "Molokini Lightstation to be Established." *Maui News,* Mar 25.

Shackleton, N. J. 1987. "Oxygen Isotopes, Ice Volume and Sea Level." *Quaternary Science Reviews* 6, 183–190.

Sherrod, David R., Yoshitomo Nishimitsu and Takahiro Tagami, 2001. "Changing Rate of Volcanism at Haleakalā, a Postshield-stage Volcano of the Hawaiian Chain." [A manuscript to be submitted to the Geological Society of America Bulletin].

Stearns, H.T., 1985. *Geology of the State of Hawai'i.* Palo Alto: Pacific Books.

Tanji, Edwin, 1984. "Molokini Blasts Rile Ma'alaea Charter Operators." *Honolulu Advertiser,* Sept. 13, B11.

Taylor, Leighton, 1993. *Sharks of Hawai'i.* Honolulu: University Of Hawai'i Press.

Tinker, Spencer W., 1982. *Fishes of Hawai'i.* Honolulu: Hawaiian Service, Inc.

Vancouver, G., 1968. *Voyage of Discovery to the North Pacific.* Vol. 2. Amsterdam: Da Capo Press.

Watson, J.S., 1961. "Feral Rabbit Populations on Pacific Islands." *Pacific Science,* 15(4).

Wray, Karl, 1945. "Molokini Described, Now Used Used as Navy Bombing Range." *Maui News,* Sept. 15, A6.

Index